HEART-THROBS

Jack Tresidder

A Golden Hands book

Marshall Cavendish, London

Picture Credits
Colour:
Camera Press pp. 17, 20, 25, 96, 105, 112, 116-117
Keystone Press Agency pp. 4-5, 21
John Kobal Collection pp. 12, 16, 24, 28, 37, 93, 97, 108, 109
Roger Morton p. 13
David Redfern pp. 8-9
State Historical Museum, Moscow p. 24
Warner Brothers Films p. 100

Black and White:
Archivo Casa Sola, Bolivar p. 120
Camera Press pp. 52, 67, 72, 88
Zoe Dominic Collection p. 85
Mary Evans Picture Library p. 64
John Kobal Collection pp. 48, 51, 55-57, 74, 76, 78, 82, 84, 86-87, 92, 98-99, 102, 109
National Film Archive pp. 6-7, 10, 14-15, 22, 27, 29, 32-36, 38-44, 46, 50, 54, 59, 63, 68, 73, 75, 77, 79, 80, 90-91, 94, 103, 106, 110, 115
Novosti Press Agency p. 119
Popperfoto p. 66-67
Radio Times Hulton Picture Library pp. 23, 26, 31, 45, 58, 69, 96, 101, 113
David Redfern pp. 61, 89
Syndication International pp. 11, 30, 49, 60, 62, 70-71, 81, 95, 107, 111
Warner Brothers Films p. 118

Front Cover:
Camera Press
John Kobal Collection
National Film Archive

Published by Marshall Cavendish Publications Limited,
58 Old Compton Street,
London W1V 5PA

©Marshall Cavendish Publications Limited 1974

This volume first published 1974

Printed by Colour Reproductions Ltd., Billericay, Essex,
and bound by R.J. Acford, Ltd., Chichester, Sussex, England.

ISBN 0 85685 069 1

This edition not to be sold in the USA,
Canada or the Philippines

About this book

If you've ever spent time day-dreaming about a heart-throb – and most of us have – then this book will give you fascinating insight into the reasons why certain men appeal. What are the special ingredients that go into making someone the object of your desires and dreams? What qualities make one man a heart-throb and another totally lacking?

The following pages contain a host of men who attract and entice women, both young and old. Each heart-throb has been described, revealing the particular assets – usually a mysterious compound of glamour and sex appeal – which have qualified him as a man who captures the romantic imagination of women of every nationality.

Probably the most important factor in producing the image of male attractiveness is the cinema. It means women can 'know' a man intimately without ever meeting him. Paul Newman has stepped into millions of women's lives through his appearance on the screen. Pop music also provides a source for the emotional fantasy of a heart-throb fan. Elvis Presley caused many an adolescent heart to palpitate through his deep, mood-making voice on records.

The ideal heart-throb of the 1970s would be lean, muscular and tallish with dark hair and heavy-lidded eyes. He would have courage and quiet confidence, and his sexual approach would be direct, almost brutal. His sensitivity would be hidden under surface hardness and his face would be lined with a hint of boyish vulnerability. His power would be latent rather than displayed.

No man possesses all these qualities, but every heart-throb in this book has some magnetic attraction, making him a figment of many women's dreams and imagination.

Muhammed Ali is the man who made Black Power beautiful. One measure of his charisma was public reaction to his defeat by Joe Frazier in March, 1971. Ali had given the public plenty of reason to dislike him. Both before and after he took the world heavyweight boxing title from Sonny Liston in 1964, he had bragged and tormented weaker opponents. He had also adopted a Black Muslim racial creed which was a spit in the eye of White America. But when Frazier beat him there was an immediate wave of public sympathy. Secretly, it seems, very few had really wanted Ali to lose. Why? Ali's style in the ring is part of the answer. "Float like a butterfly, sting like a bee", he said. His combination of pantherish force and balletic grace, his compact good-looks, the muscled sheen of his skin, the lightning speed of his reflexes and the crispness of his punching were a contrast with the slugging and shambling of almost every other boxer in heavyweight history.

Added to this is the fascination of a boyish ego in a man's body. Ali can be dim and witty, oafish and charming, silly and wise, boastful and humble. Particularly in the early years of his ring career when he used his speed to pull his unguarded head away from blows, he looked like an amateur who had climbed through the ropes on some kind of horrific dare. He seemed to be tempting fate to hurt him. And it may be this idea of Ali's that he can shape events his way simply by willing it, that explains his attraction for people who are stuck with whatever destiny hands out to them.

Ali always believed he would be world champion. He was born Cassius Marcellus Clay at Louisville, U.S.A. in January, 1942, son of a proud but frustrated painter who told him "You'll never be rich; look at the colour of your skin". Cassius did not see college as a way to the top and decided at 12 to learn boxing. He won the Olympic light-heavyweight title at Rome in 1960 and began

Muhammed Ali has a far reaching fascination for admirers and critics alike. His fights with Frazier in 1971 and 1974 are among the greatest in history.

leaping, laughing and shouting wildly about how he would be heavyweight champion in four years. To make it happen, he gave uncanny predictions about the outcome of his fights – "If he gives me jive, he'll fall in five". And when, sure enough, he did beat a confused Liston in February, 1964, it looked almost as if he had conned his way to the top.

The serious side of Ali's character emerged over the next few years when he joined the Black Muslims but turned down the US Army ("I got no fight with those Viet Congs"). His strict beliefs led him to put aside his first wife, Chicago model Sonji Roi, and to a three and a half-year suspension from boxing. The long lay-off slowed the reflex speed which had always been crucial to his boxing and at the end of the comeback trail, Joe Frazier was waiting with a hook which lifted him right off his feet. Another man might have looked undignified. Ali

Dr Christian Barnard, focus of medical controversy and public acclaim since 1967 when he transplanted the first human heart in his native South Africa.

hung on stubbornly to lose a tremendous battle on points and then said, "I never thought of losing, but now that it's happened, the only thing is to do it right. If so-called great people can take these defeats without cracking, the others are encouraged. They feel strong". It is the authentic hero's stance: Fate can be beaten.

Christian Barnard: No man has ever become a heartthrob faster or with more ironic aptness. Christian Barnard, born in 1923, son of a hard-up Dutch Reformed Church minister, was almost unknown outside his native South Africa until December, 1967, when he carried out the first transplant of a human heart. His patient, Louis Washansky, survived only 18 days. But by then, the surgeon who headed the transplant team at Groot Schuur hospital was a celebrity.

The mystique of a medical miracle-worker is a fundamental part of Barnard's public appeal. His autobiography provides several other clues. It reveals a strong will to win (he wept after losing a schoolboy race and at one stage in his career, dropped everything in an attempt to make his daughter world champion water skier), a consuming energy (which enabled him to work on experimental veterinary research until 4 a.m. after a full day's work in hospital), and an unusual sensitivity. Far from being worn out by 25 years of unpublicized medical slogging, Barnard confronted the world's cameras in 1967 tall and bronzed with deep-set green eyes, chiselled features, a sensual mouth and plenty of white teeth. He looked almost too good to be true. And all this overt sex appeal was completed by a frank admiration for women which flowered almost the moment he became a social lion.

His first wife, Louwtjie, whom he had met in 1945 and with whom he set up a country GP practice before going to America to study heart surgery in the 1950s, has said he did not have the character to withstand the pressures of fame. But Dr Barnard is unrepentant about the two years of globe-trotting and cocktail parties which took him away from his wife and two children after the first transplant operation. In the process of publicising heart research, he claims he did no more than other men in their mid-40s secretly want to do. Princesses, socialites, actresses and international beauties fell at his feet and he made the most of it. Louwtjie divorced him, and in 1970, at the age of 47, he married a 19-year-old heiress, Barbara Zoellner.

More recently, Barnard has settled down to dedicated surgical work in Capetown and has taken up courageous political stands against apartheid. He survived both a threat of rheumatoid arthritis and a serious accident in 1972. Women are susceptible in greater or lesser degree to most doctors. Christian Barnard had a combination of charm, success and looks which could hardly fail to turn heads, including, perhaps, his own.

John Barrymore, "the Great Profile", (1882-1942) was the only man to become a matinee idol of stage, silent films and also talkies. He was the younger brother of Ethel and Lionel, dropped a career as an illustrator to join them on the stage in 1903 and by 1920, when he played Richard II, was thought the finest Shakespearean actor of his day.

In 1925 he swapped fame for notoriety, went to Hollywood and became what he called "a silly, scented jackass", spoofing his way through films like "Don Juan" in which he set a kissing record (191). Though his high forehead, pale classical features and splendid Roman nose could have made him a rival to Valentino, he had too much sardonic humour to make a convincing screen lover. He made up for this off-screen, becoming a compulsive seducer who finally married, at 54, a girl of 19 who came to interview him at a clinic where he was drying out after a drinking bout. The girl, Elaine Jacobs, was his fourth wife. His third, Dolores Costello, was said to have fainted under his kisses in "The Sea Beast" which they filmed together in 1925. For Dolores, whom he married in 1928, Barrymore built one of Hollywood's most lavish mansions, later boarding up many rooms so that no secret lover could ravish her. As well as being insanely jealous, he had a superstitious fear of going mad, as his father had, and behaved as if determined to forestall this by drinking himself to death.

Though his alcoholism increasingly affected his acting, Barrymore was still drawing full houses in 1939 when he toured in "My Dear Children". He saw through his own vanity ("I'm 50 years old and I want to look like Jackie Cooper's grandson") and played the role of eccentric to the hilt, keeping a pet vulture named Maloney, surrounding himself with a group of ageing Bohemians and delighting the public with his cynical ad-libbing. He once flung a fish at a coughing audience and shouted: "Busy yourselves with that, you damned walruses, while the rest of us proceed with the play". The public forgave him everything – perhaps because Barrymore could not take his own decadence any more seriously than he had taken his talent.

Left John Barrymore poses elegantly in a bedroom
scene from his 1926 film "Don Juan" in which he set a
new Hollywood kissing record. Reviewers were
impressed by his "luminous, decadent profile". But
the cheap settings, grotesque costumes and adolescent
plots of films like this shocked admirers of his
distinguished stage career. Only four years earlier,
his performance of Hamlet had been hailed by some
critics as a definitive portrayal of the moody prince.
Right Alan Bates, bearded for the role of Birkin in
Ken Russell's film, "Women in Love", in which Bates
becomes one of the first British actors to undress
on the screen without looking self-conscious.

Alan Bates' versatility as an actor has prevented him being typecast as a British sex symbol and he has yet to make a film with the kind of vogue appeal that might make him a superstar. But after beginning quietly in nice-fellow roles, Bates is emerging as something lustier. Compare the inhibited Englishman he played in "Zorba the Greek" (1965) with Birkin of "Women in Love" (1969), or the rampant rustic of "The Go-Between" (1971). His appeal is based on a mobile face, now creasing attractively under thick brown hair, and a particularly bold stare from greenish eyes. He was born in England in Allestree, Derbyshire in 1934, nursed acting ambitions when at school and went to the Royal Academy of Dramatic Art after service in the RAF. He moved into films in 1960 after a series of outstanding performances at London's Royal Court theatre. He married in 1970.

The Beatles were a schizoid dream – four personalities in one. Other singing groups have had a collective magnetism, notably the Rolling Stones, but none seemed as mysteriously unified as the Beatles. Was it only coincidence that this entertainment phenomenon arose in the 1960s, the same decade in which the idea of group love began to catch on?

John Lennon, Paul McCartney and George Harrison have all taken their separate talents and individuality into the 1970s, but none of them projects the glamour of the four-sided personality that was the Beatles. The elements that made it up give some clues to its attraction: Bossiness, arrogance, a streak of cruel wit (John); imagination, high-spirits, polite irreverence (Paul); dependability, practicality (George); gentleness, sentimentality (Ringo). Add to all this, a driving Mersey beat, four tossing mops of shiny-clean hair and the fact that the Beatles were

working-class boys skylarking their way through all the hysteria and adulation with a matter-of-fact air. What emerges is a compendium image of 1960s youth as it wanted to see itself. The Beatles were a narcissistic dream of what every boy-next-door could be.

The biographical data supports their ''ordinariness''. All were born in Liverpool of humble parents, Richard (Ringo) Starkey in July and John Lennon in October, 1940, Paul McCartney in June 1942, George Harrison in February 1943. Only Ringo, who was an apprentice fitter, and John, who did part of an art college course, flirted with other occupations than entertaining. None was at all impressed by school and John and George were actively rebellious. Paul, though smart, was obsessed with the guitar from the age of 15 when he turned to it after his mother died. John also lost his mother when he was 17 and both he and Ringo were the product of marriages which broke up while they were babies.

So the optimistic message the Beatles brought to the

1960s was that you could become a success without either of the two things usually held to be essential – background or academic honours. You could get to the top just by being yourself. Nobody could even say the Beatles' success was stage-managed by shrewd publicity manipulators. They had a fanatical following in Liverpool in 1960 before the rest of the world knew about them and their first hit ''Love Me Do'', reached the top by public demand rather than disc-jockey plugging. They thought up the name Beatles themselves (suggested by Buddy Holly and the Crickets) and their hair style was created by a friend in Hamburg.

Their manager, Brian Epstein, ''cleaned up'' their image of course and their fans began to mould it to their own wishes in the mid 1960s. Neil Aspinell, their road manager, said: ''They've always come across as being so good and kind and nice when they're not really, not more than other people. I think people wanted them to be like that''. But in the main, the Beatles made it themselves.

The Beatles at a Press conference during the ''flower-power'' era of their ''Magical Mystery Tour''. Under the casual balloon of high spirits lay musical genius – a new style and attitude towards music resulted from the talents of the Beatles. Their sense of carefree fun, spontaneity and naturalness contributed to their appeal.

And to the public their highly original musical and verbal talents seemed less important ingredients of their success than their confidence and their infectious, mischievous, natural personalities. Though this was largely an illusion, they were adored because they seemed ''amateur'' and spontaneous in a frighteningly complex world. They were also a uniquely multiple heart-throb. Girls didn't know whether they were squealing at the rich blue of Ringo's eyes or the soft brown of Paul's, the brooding concentration of George or the extrovert frenzy of John. As Paul McCartney said: ''The thing is, we're all really the same person.''

Warren Beatty made his film debut in "Splendour in the Grass" in 1961, and was hailed as a major new star who combined the explosive force of Brando with the charm of a little boy lost. According to *Time* magazine, he was "arrogant, attractive, hostile, moody, sensitive, self-conscious, bright, defensive, ambitious, stuttering, self-seeking and extremely talented". He had been selected by director Elia Kazan to succeed James Dean as a cult figure of psychiatric delinquency. And Kazan himself was later to call him "the sexiest guy in the cinema business today".

Beatty, the younger brother of actress Shirley MacLaine, born at Richmond, Virginia in 1937, was a football star and a "cheerful hypocrite" (his own description) at school and made a rapid impression on Broadway before moving to Hollywood. Apart from his green-blue eyes, his shock of dark brown hair and his self-amused expression, the key to his personal magnetism is a quality of latent tension in his acting. Behind the off-screen image of a wayward philanderer who had well-publicised affairs with other men's wives was a young man with independent and original ideas of film-making. His "Bonnie and Clyde" (1967) established a new cinematic style.

Beatty's performance in this film with Faye Dunaway made Bonnie and Clyde the most unlikely folk heroes in history. He advanced the novel idea that killers might simply be silly kids making whoopee. Beatty's combination of superficial gaiety and snake-like menace make him the supreme hip actor. His message seems to be that no matter what a man does, he's a hero if he does it with enough style.

Warren Beatty as Clyde Barrow, the hip gangster hero of "Bonnie and Clyde" (1967). At the climax of the film he drives into a hail of bullets with Faye Dunaway.

arry Belafonte: "From the top of his head right down to that white shirt, he's the most beautiful man I've ever seen", said Diahann Caroll. Standing there in his tight black trousers, seaman's belt and half-open Indian cotton shirt, hands moving expressively under a mauve spotlight, with his chiselled head thrown back, his eyes half closed and that high, husky voice floating, Harry Belafonte had a potent sex appeal that few other singers, black or white, have ever approached.

He was the first Negro heart-throb, the first man to cross the romantic colour lines in a film (when Joan Fontaine fell for him in "Island in the Sun") and the first man to sell a million LP discs ("Belafonte Sings of the Caribbean"). Born in New York of Jamaican parents in 1927, he was an actor, ran a Greenwich Village restaurant and was an unsuccessful jazz singer in the late 1940s, tried again with folk songs in the early 50s and became a celebrity when he starred in "Carmen Jones" in 1955. His early struggle and his hatred of race

Harry Belafonte, the citizen-star whose arrangements of West Indian folk music made him the biggest selling singer of the mid-1950s. His popularity was so great that he broke through racial barriers as a film star.

prejudice produced an emotional tension that reflected itself in the dramatic magnetism of his stage personality. His combination of 6ft 2in. muscularity and elegance and the range of his untrained, musky voice could mesmerise audiences.

Belafonte was intelligent enough to avoid being typecast by the calypso boom he launched in the mid-50s. He stayed out of films for 10 years after 1959, used television and the night-club circuits judiciously to avoid over-exposure, and remains a superstar. He has two children by his first marriage which ended in 1957 and a son, David, by his marriage to Julie Robinson, who was the only white dancer in the Katherine Dunham company. Apart from his pioneering work in collecting folk music, Belafonte has been prominent in civil rights and education and was on the governing board of the Peace Corps.

11

Jean-Paul Belmondo, one of the few European film stars who has been able to win an international reputation as a virile and attractive male without moving outside his own country's film industry.

Jean-Paul Belmondo is France's compendium answer to Douglas Fairbanks, Humphrey Bogart, Steve McQueen and anyone who thinks Frenchmen are cissy. Belmondo became an international addiction in the mid-1960s when students discovered that in addition to being a good film actor, he had been hit over the head by that bête noire of revolutionary youth, a Parisian policeman. Though he had been abusing the police for slow service to an injured motor-cyclist rather than for fascist piggery, it was enough that Belmondo had tangled with the law. He was fined for bad language but successfully sued the policeman who clubbed him.

He is 6ft of sinewy, kinetic energy with an attractively-ugly face which looks as if it has recently emerged from a punch-up. In his youth, it often had. His enthusiasm for amateur boxing left him with a squashed nose. Born in April, 1933, at Neuilly-sur-Seine on the outskirts of Paris, he was the son of an academic sculptor. He rebelled against his elegant background, was

expelled from some of the best schools in France and at 26, electrified French audiences as the tough, flip young man of Jean-Luc Godard's film "Breathless". Godard's wife said "He's not handsome, but at least he's vulgar". France was hard-up for heroes and Belmondo's zest for physical sensation became legendary. He drove fast cars, did his own stunt work even when it involved hurtling off a cliff at 80 m.p.h. on a motor-cycle. Though he stuck to his dancer wife, Elodie, and his three children, Belmondo otherwise projected a maverick image, irreverent, easygoing and abrasive to authority. He strikes outsiders as more representative of French virility than any of his better-looking fellow actors.

George Best, the temperamental genius of Manchester United announced in 1972 that he was fed up with football and flew off to the fleshpots of Majorca. But as the super-babe of soccer in the 1960s, Best was the most adored player in the history of the game in Britain. His vivid blue eyes and tangle of black hair made him as popular with girls as with their football-mad brothers, gasping at his brilliance and audacity on the field. Best was born in Northern Ireland in 1946. He was a short, skinny nine-stone boy when he was brought to England by a talent scout in 1963 and after a homesick flight back to Ireland was persuaded to make a career of football in Manchester. His wispiness concealed deceptive strength and speed. He also had courage, no nerves, and a natural ball-control like that of the great Brazilian player, Pele. After he scored two goals in Lisbon at the age of 19, he became an idol, harassed on the field by the rough tactics of more mediocre players and off it by swarms of girls. By the 1971 season he was swollenheaded, jaded and resentful of management discipline. The Press had a field-day when he was suspended for spending a weekend with an actress instead of playing. In 1972 there were more sudden disappearances with beauties (including Miss Great Britain, Carolyne Moore), another suspension, a brief "retirement" in Spain and finally a parting with football.

During a nine-month lay-off in 1973, Best grew sleek in plush foreign resorts, negotiated the launching of a nightclub in Manchester, was involved in a fracas or two, and finally confessed that he missed football, missed the adulation and had sometimes acted like an adolescent. He returned to football and was greeted like a prodigal son. Though he is not the steadiest player in the game, nobody else has his ability to surprise and delight and so far as women are concerned, nobody looks as good either.

George Best, super-babe of British football in the 1960s, in Majorca during one of his truancies from the game. Talent and good looks were no armour against the pressures of publicity and public idolatry.

irk Bogarde's astonishing performance in Visconti's "Death in Venice" (1973) confirmed that he is a screen actor of great subtlety. His reign as an idol of teenage girls (top of the British box office in 1955 and 1957) was more puzzling at least to Bogarde himself. But Bogarde had the same attraction that many of today's pop-stars have. He was a refuge from all that he-man virility of stars like Gable. The slight build, the sensual mouth, the delicately raised left eyebrow, the sensitive, rather anguished face, was neither wholly masculine or feminine. There was a hint of delicious cruelty (he's marvellous at playing villains) and at the same time of motherable softness.

Though he always looked 10 years younger, Dirk Bogarde was born in London in 1920, son of a Dutch art correspondent. He himself trained as an artist and designer but switched to acting in 1939 and continued his stage career after war service. He has been acting in films and plays since 1948, was an enormous success in the "Doctor in the House" series, made several fine films exploring homosexual themes in the 1960s and is now living in semi-retirement in France.

Dirk Bogarde looking typically suave in a scene from John Schlesinger's 1965 film, "Darling". His performance as the long-suffering lover of Julie Christie won him a British Film Academy Award.

umphrey Bogart was always popular during his 26-year film career, yet nobody would have expected "Bogey" to become a cult hero 10 years after his death. But there his photograph was, pinned on the walls of student flats, with his prison-cropped hair and rough stubble jaw, his tight, seamed face and stark eyes, a cigarette drooping from his scarred lip. Someone once described him as the masculine counterpart of the soft-hearted prostitute. And Bogart himself said: "My own experience with heels of the first order has been that they universally attract women". To the anti-war generation of the late 1960s, Bogart was the ideal anti-hero – a man committed only to himself and hiding his compassion under a shell of harsh talk and often lawless action.

Humphrey De Forest Bogart (1899-1957) was the son of a prominent New York surgeon, once appeared in an advertisement for baby food, and began his stage career playing good-looking gentlemanly roles. But the streak of toughness was always there. He had been a high-spirited boy who didn't like school and had enlisted as soon as he could in the Navy where a splinter of wood from an exploding shell gave him his invaluable twisted grin and lisp. World War I over, he began to work for a friend as a stage-manager and then as a juvenile lead. Interspersed with some early films and two short-lived marriages, his stage career continued until 1936 when his chilling portrayal of Duke Mantee in "The Petrified Forest" led to the same role in the film and a permanent move to Hollywood.

For the next six years he played gangsters, usually dying in a hail of bullets. But in 1941 with "High Sierra" and "The Maltese Falcon", the Bogartian hero began to emerge – a man still outside society but obeying a personal code of honour, strong on loyalty and ready to mete out his own justice. He appeared to be a cynic – "I stick my neck out for nobody", he told Ingrid Bergman in "Casablanca" (1943). But again and again, the hardness, the neutrality, the flippancy, would crumble and reveal courage, integrity, tenderness.

The off-screen Bogart seemed to mesh with the characters he was now playing. His 1938 marriage to a tough little actress Mayo Methot (he called her "Sluggy") was Hollywood's stormiest love-match. They drank and brawled happily together until 1944. Neighbours were kept awake by the sound of breaking crockery. "This kid is madly in love with me", Bogart would say, side-stepping a plate and grinning wolfishly. "I've got colour. I live dangerously." According to one nightclub owner he once arrived at the club bleeding from a stab wound in the back he had not even noticed Mayo deliver. "Bogart's a helluver nice guy until 11.30 p.m." said another. "After that, he starts thinking he's Bogart." The Battling Bogarts split up soon after he met Lauren Bacall (Betty Joan Perske), his co-star in "To Have and Have Not" (1944). She was 18, Bogart, 45. "If you want me, just whistle'', she said, and he did. They married in 1947, had a son and daughter, and settled down as the centre of the Holmby Hills rat-pack, a hard-drinking, wise-cracking group of friends. Bogart began reaching out for a wider range of acting roles and won an Academy Award for ''The African Queen'' (1952). Early in 1956 he survived a massive operation for throat cancer and fought bitterly to recover. But on January 12 the following year he said ''Goodbye kid'' to Bacall and drifted into a coma.

The camp nostalgia for Bogart's trench coat, his grating voice and his mannerisms, is partly a nostalgia for the era of the 1940s itself. Because he espoused liberal

Humphrey Bogart of the tough shell and sad eyes – a photograph taken in the early 1950s. He liked to begin a friendship with a provocative insult.

causes off-screen and was a sceptic who displayed contempt for authority in his film roles as well, Bogart is one of the few stars ''modern'' enough for the taste of a later generation of film-goers. He is therefore a way back into a world less complex than our own. But the Bogartian type also has a lasting fascination for women. He looked sinister and could be rough. ''When you're slapped you'll take it and like it'', says Sam Spade in ''The Maltese Falcon''. In a way, he was the ugly, bad-tempered reality many women have to live with. But he was never really frightening. Women could see through his toughness. And while he was always master of the physical situation, he was prepared to treat women as equals and give it to them straight. Judging by his continuing popularity, a lot of women are prepared to trade conventional romance for a solid chunk of Bogart's integrity.

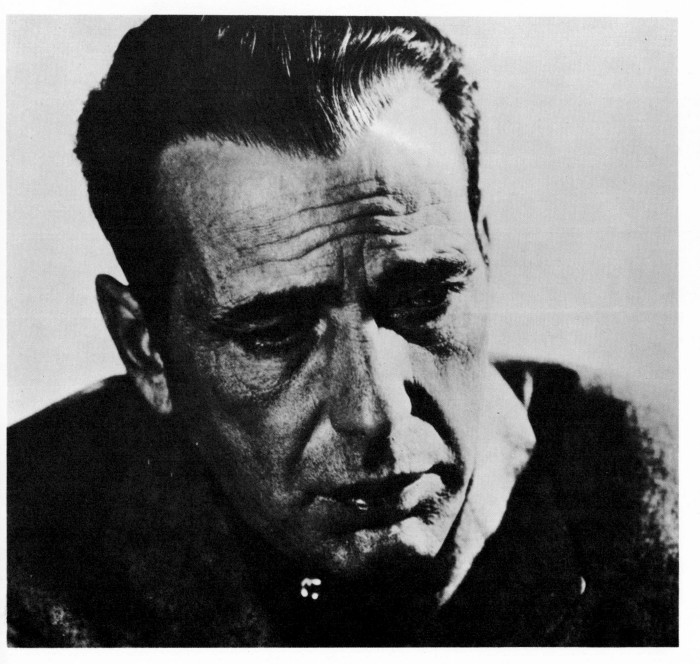

*J*ames Bond. Agent 007. Ex-naval commander, now senior licensed killer for British Secret Service. Tall, slim, black-haired, blue-eyed, scar down right cheek, longish nose, wide, finely-drawn but rather cruel mouth, firm jaw, preference for dark-blue Sea Island sleeveless shirts or dark suits with black knitted ties, steel-capped boots and .25 Beretta in shoulder holster. Scottish parents. Chelsea address (when not travelling). Widower (wife Tracy lasted only 1½ hours). No children. Heavy smoker, fussy eater and drinker. Unusual pain tolerance. Social loner. Expert with knives, fists, cars, explosives, women. Irresistible even to lesbians. Highly promiscuous – but who wouldn't be when recipient of invitations like this: "I want it all James. Everything you've ever done to a girl. Now. Quickly."

Author Ian Fleming who blew Bond's cover in his first novel, *Casino Royale*, in 1953, described him as "ruthless and self-indulgent but not a bad man". The best-known screen Bond, Sean Connery, also defends him against charges that he is a sad and rather ignorant sado-masochist without ideals, morals or friends. Connery points out that Bond is not an adulterer, kills only to survive and is forced by the nature of his job to reduce everything to the verbs to sniff, look, listen, taste, think. To him, Bond is the "invincible superman all men would like to copy, all women would like to conquer". Bond's women speak of his "sweet brutality", his "rather cold passion". They are often drawn to him under the stress of danger, even torture. There's seldom any mention of love or marriage. And perhaps here we have the clue to Bond's charisma for both women and men. He triumphs equally over pain, death and marital boredom. He is the ultimate fantasy, the great sexual survivor.

*C*harles Boyer's heavy-lidded brown eyes, the fluttering vein in his temple, his raised eyebrow, his caressing smile and the light, throbbing quality of his accented bass voice were the epitome of Continental charm as Hollywood saw it. He never did say "Come wiz me to zee Casbah" in "Algiers" (1938) but the line became a legend used by every comedian who wanted to parody French techniques of love. Nobody has ever been able to better the air of bored worldliness with which Boyer attracted a succession of female stars ranging from Garbo to Ingrid Bergman. Though he was still projecting senior allure in the television series "The Rogues" in the late 1960s, Boyer was born in 1899. At 18, he left his home town of Figeac, near Bordeaux, to study at the Paris Conservatory. When he appeared on the French stage in 1921 he became a matinee idol almost overnight. He moved to Hollywood in 1931 and stayed quietly married to the English girl, Pat Patterson, whom he met three years after arriving in Hollywood.

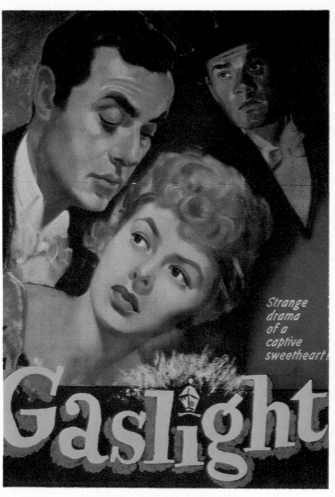

Charles Boyer as he appeared in a 1944 poster for "Gaslight", one of the many films he made during this period opposite Ingrid Bergman. The "Com wiz me to zee Casbah" line is identified with him.

*M*arlon Brando loves a practical joke. It may be only zany humour that makes him sometimes book into second-class hotels as "Lord Greystoke". On the other hand, it may provide a clue to his otherwise baffling personality. "Lord Greystoke" was the title claimed by that castaway son of an English aristocrat, Tarzan (see page 108). And Brando shares with Tarzan more than a powerful build and a tendency to grunt – namely a deep mistrust of human society. Both on and off the screen, Brando often seems to see himself as a modern personification of Edgar Rice Burrough's fantasy – a natural man at bay in a hostile world of pseudo-civilization and yearning for the old simplicities of the jungle. Asked in "The Wild One" (1954) what he is rebelling against,

Marlon Brando, maturing well, twenty years after his explosive film debut as Stanley Kowalski in "A Streetcar Named Desire". He set a new trend in acting and is the most imitated actor of the post-war era.

Brando retorts in a classic gesture of defiance, ''What have you got?'' His you-name-it-I'll-fight-it attitude, his protean acting talent and his sheer physical magnetism made him the superstar hero of a rebellious generation.

Brando's forebears were French (Brandeau). He was born in Omaha in 1924. His mother was interested in theatre, his father sold chemicals. Marlon was spoiled, misbehaved at school and was expelled from a military academy just before his graduation in 1943. Elia Kazan, the director he most admires, gave him acting lessons in New York, he got his first Broadway part in 1944 and after some time off to travel and study, he took on the role that made him famous – Stanley Kowalski in ''A Streetcar named Desire''. Brando made Kowalski a completely original slob-sex-symbol. Mumbling, scratching, staring, belching and bawling, he projected an animal sensuality which over-rode the brutishness of the character and made him seem more sexually attractive than repulsive. In the 1952 film version, in his smouldering portrayal of Zapata (1952), in ''The Wild One'' and in his Oscar-winning performance as Terry Malloy in ''On the Waterfront'' (1954), the Brando style was rounded out. It has had many imitators but the original has never been equalled. Physically, Brando's presence in his films of the early 1950s is one of overwhelming virility. The arrogance and pugnacity of the wide-backed, muscular body, the jutting brows and nose and the impression of a stored ferocity is all set off by a broad, lofty forehead which seems to heighten his power by contradicting everything else.

The sweat-stained T-shirt he wore in ''Streetcar'' and his black leather jacket in ''The Wild One'' reinforced the aura of primitive toughness. But what made him so appealing to his own generation was that his brooding intensity, his swagger and his bouts of violent loutishness always seemed to hide a ''little-boy'' quality of confusion. He rebelled against authority but was not able to rationalise and control everything like the remote heroes of the past. Teenagers could identify with the stubborn integrity of Terry Malloy in ''On the Waterfront'', finally standing up to the syndicate with the support of a tender girl.

Brando's problem as an actor has been how to break away from an image that corresponded so closely with his own real-life personality. Until 1972 when his talents found powerful new expression in ''The Godfather'' and ''Last Tango in Paris'', his films were never quite as successful as he hoped. He gave middling performances in middling comedies, became known as a box-office risk through his moodiness on the sets of more serious films, and often seemed to be doing self-parodies of the inarticulate Brando style. Off-screen, Brando's insecurity became legendary. He ate compulsively, spent money recklessly. He went about in torn shirts and dirty sneakers. He took to wearing FBI-type disguises. He nursed childhood neuroses (waspishly revealed by Truman Capote in an unauthorized interview). He sulked if he felt other actors or actresses were upstaging him. He insisted on making all his roles highly sympathetic (including the Nazi in ''The Young Lions''). He delighted in masochistic roles like the one he played in his own film ''One-Eyed Jacks''. He boasted of his ability to have any woman he wanted and sometimes seemed to like humiliating them.

All this, said the amateur psychiatrists, was the guilty reaction of a young man who had found himself an overnight success despite a naughty childhood, a limited academic background and few social graces. Perhaps they were partly right. Brando has often said he regards acting as a neurotic and unworthy trade which he follows purely in order to earn money for a ''more meaningful life''. By this, he means mainly working for minority groups, joining marches, giving money and speaking up for civil rights. Cynics see this as a further extension of the Brando ego rather than any deep or thoughtful commitment. But his distrust of authority and affection for the weak seem genuine. So does his feeling for the children of his marriages to Anna Kashfi (1957-59) and the Mexican actress Movita (1960-61), as well as of his liaison with Tarita, his Tahitian co-star in ''Mutiny on the Bounty'' (he has an exotic taste in women). Yet Brando remains the greatest film actor of his time. And though admirers of his talent may deplore his vanity, his self-destructive temperament and his inability to find himself, his chaotic personal life has done little harm to his status as the dominant sex hero of a chaotic post-war era.

Rossano Brazzi said: 'Women are like guitars. . just look into their eyes and work down from there''. Publicity like this, in combination with sleepy blue eyes, crinkly hair greying at the temples, suave charm and his heavy Italian accent made him the Great Lover of the 1950s – the answer to America's hunger for a taste of lush Latin gallantry in a wilderness of unromantic sex. Brazzi's screen ardour was convincing enough to produce a fan mail of 5000 letters a week and scenes of mild hysteria among middle-aged women when he appeared in public. But though his languid charm was sincere, the passion was an illusion. Apart from ''Summer Madness'' with Katherine Hepburn in 1954, Mr Brazzi had little time for his films or his romantic image. He remained happily married to his plump, jolly childhood sweetheart, Lydia, and quietly salted away enough money to build his own production studios in Italy. Born in 1916, he has a Florence law degree, has appeared in nearly 200 Italian films and confesses to being – so far as romance goes – quite the opposite of the Latin stereotype he once represented in Hollywood.

Rossano Brazzi with Katherine Hepburn in his best film, ''Summer Madness'', a moving study of middle-age passion between an American woman and a Venetian.

Jim Brown with Raquel Welch, his co-star, in "100 Rifles". Although not suitable for audiences in South Africa, the film broke new ground elsewhere.

im Brown is the first Negro with the potential to become a screen sex hero. He has moved some way into the dangerous territory that has divided black and white sexuality in the popular cinema. At 6ft 2in and 16 stone, he is a massive and formidable screen personality. In "100 Rifles", the cultural shock of his semi-nude clinches with Raquel Welch was softened by making her a half-caste. But Brown has nevertheless been able to project black virility more aggressively than Sidney Poitier. Born in the U.S.A. in 1936, he is still best-known to his hometown as the former star fullback of the Cleveland Browns football team.

Yul Brynner is the most comforting sex symbol balding men have ever known. He shaved his handsomely-moulded skull to play "The King and I" on Broadway in 1951 and after one or two brief regrowths, accepted his destiny as scourge of the hair-transplant business. His screen sex appeal is based on old-style male autocracy – all bulging muscles, cracking whips and curling lips. When not wielding a curved sword or bullying his Siamese subjects, he usually totes guns and wears black. Though nearing 60, he has lost little of the animal force and magnetism that won him an Oscar for the 1956 film version of "The King and I". Part of his attractiveness is that for all his flaring nostrils and popping eyes he manages to suggest that he is capable of being wrapped around little female fingers. Brynner's exoticism is genuine. He was born in Siberia in 1915, and studied in Paris, worked in France as a trapeze artist and life-guard, taught himself enough English to play Shakespeare soon after coming to America in 1941, and was in and out of radio, television and stage musicals until his career took off in 1951. He married for the third time in 1971.

Yul Brynner, despair of the toupee business, in Rome during the filming of a recent Western. His Oscar-winning performance in "The King and I" launched him into the public eye as a man with magnetism and appeal.

21

Richard Burton at bay in "Who's Afraid of Virginia Woolf", the 1966 film version of Albee's play about an American academic and his shrew-like wife.

Richard Burton not only can afford to buy enormous diamonds for Elizabeth Taylor but also looks as if he has personally mined them. His green eyes glitter bleakly in a face like a seam of pitted rock. At the height of his career as an actor, he was the aggressive male personified, a man of such dominant physical and mental power that he could call himself "diabolically famous" and not seem to be bragging. There have been better actors than Burton and bigger stars. But in the history of show business there has seldom been quite such a celebrity.

Nobody would have found it easy to stay on the pinnacle the Burtons reached between 1963 and 1967 when public resentment of their love affair gave way to adulation and everything they touched turned to gold. (Their income one year was about £4 million). By 1971, overexposure of their lavish, hard-drinking living style

had brought them high on *Time* magazine's list of famous bores. But ten years earlier, *Time* had hailed Burton as "Mr Box Office". And 20 years earlier, when Burton played Prince Hal at Stratford, Kenneth Tynan had praised him for his quality of brimming stillness, his dark, unwinking eyes and urgent voice, his ability to show the "mystery and power of which heroes are capable". There are those who believe Burton has wasted that great acting talent. Claire Bloom, who played opposite his superb Leamas in "The Spy Who Came In From The Cold" thinks he has become boring because he has got what he always wanted – fame and fortune. But on the stage, on the screen and, most of all, in the flesh, Burton has had a magnetic attraction for both men and women ever since he was a tough, bull-chested boy in the coal-black village of Pontrhydyfen, South Wales.

He was born there in November, 1925, the 12th child of a barmaid, who died when he was two, and of a miner named Dick Jenkins, a little terrier of a man who loved his drink. Richard Walter Jenkins changed his name to Burton at 16 when Philip Burton, a school-teacher, rescued him from a job in a men's outfitters, sent him back to school and began training the immense acting talent he already detected in him. At 18, Emlyn Williams put him into the cast of a play called "The Druid's Rest" and a critic said he showed "exceptional ability". At 19, while he was serving three years in the RAF, he went to Oxford on a short course and Professor Neville Coghill reported, "This boy is a genius and will be a great actor. He is outstandingly handsome and robust, very masculine, with deep inward fire and extremely reserved". Burton's years as a rumbustious bachelor, drinking, fighting and Rugby-playing, ended in 1948 when he married a drama student, Sybil Williams.

On stage, the peaks of his career have been his Prince Hal in 1951, his Henry V in 1955, his King Arthur in "Camelot" (1960) and his Hamlet in 1964. But despite two forays to Hollywood during the 1950s, it was not until 1958 in "Look Back in Anger" that he found a film role which really expressed his aggressive personality. His best screen roles since then have all had the same quality of seared bitterness. He has never been a romantic "star". There is something too virile and self-contained about his acting, some lonely, withdrawn quality that prevents him making emotional contact with his co-stars. In his worst films, he projects little more than a kind of bad-tempered woodenness. As a male personality however, his tumbling gift of words and the force of his wide-set green eyes, his big, solid head and barrel chest are overwhelming. Elizabeth Taylor called his attraction a "jungle essence". There are conflicting legends of how he began the love affair during the filming of "Cleopatra" (1962) that would break up her marriage to Eddie Fisher and his much deep-rooted marriage to Sybil Burton. According to one version, Burton crushed her grand entrance on to the set by whispering: "You're too fat". Elizabeth Taylor's own story is that she was attracted not by his pugnacity but by his vulnerability.

Burton's bleak strength, the resources of his harsh, electrifying voice, are one side of his appeal for women. The other is a kind of accusing pathos – the look of a defiant, whipped boy who has been behaving badly and thinks nobody loves him. In fact, of course, he was at one time a formidable lady-killer. Producer Frank Ross called him "a born male coquette". Like most larger-than-life men, Burton is a compulsive teller of tall tales and carries about him the whiff of self-destruction. Part of the continuing fascination of a precarious Burton double-act since he and Elizabeth Taylor married in 1964 has been to see how long these two great sex symbols can sustain their myth and their imperial living style without a palace revolution.

Lord Byron, (1788-1824) one of scores of good-looking poets who have been devastatingly attractive to women, was the most romantic of them all. Amorous scandal surrounded him from the moment he returned to England from wandering abroad in 1811 and began publishing the first cantos of *Childe Harold*. An adulterous affair with Lady Caroline Lamb (who smuggled herself into his rooms dressed as a page) was succeeded by stories of his coarse behaviour towards his wife, Annabelle Milbanke – a prudish heiress who left him soon after their marriage in 1815, complaining that he seemed to prefer his own half-sister, Augusta. Rejecting the hypocrisy of London society, Byron went to Switzerland where a young woman named Claire Clairmont pursued him and bore him a daughter. A year or two later there was fresh gossip as he began a long liaison with the beautiful Teresa Guiccioli, wife of an Italian count. His frank sensuality fed rumours of bisexual orgies as well. A Greek youth was the passion of Byron's last months at Missolonghi, where he died of a fever while organizing a mercenary army to help free Greece from Turkish rule.

Byron's promiscuity (a travelling companion describes him falling upon his chambermaid "like a thunderbolt") is usually attributed to childhood anxieties created by his mother whose taunts of "lame brat" made him hypersensitive about his slightly-deformed foot. By his own count, some 200 other women found Byron's lustrous brown eyes, olive skin and classic profile irresistible. Rebelliousness was in his blood. He was the grandson of a notorious "wicked lord" and the son of a charming profligate. A man of courage and wit as well as great poetic gifts, Byron is one of the few English writers who have left an enduring legend in Europe.

Lord Byron as one of his contemporaries imagined him, communing with his muse on an Italian mountain top.

*Michael Caine, Cockney connoisseur of clothes,
antiques and women. Actress Faye Dunaway said he
had an attractive air of "moving on".*

Michael Caine said about himself "I rose to
popularity on a tide of fashionable vulgarity". This
typically self-mocking assessment of his own career, has
a good deal of truth. The screen Caine is a Cockney
boy-next-door, moving from girl to girl with a rabbity grin,
not making any of the pretences to morality or courage of
the old-style hero. With his wavy hair and long-lashed
eyes, Caine has a raffish, slightly myopic charm which
came across effectively in "Alfie" (1966). Alfie is a
chatty, amusing cad whom women should dislike for his
utter selfishness. In fact they can't resist him because
he's too frank and too natural. He is not too different
from Mr Caine himself. Shelley Winters called him "the
sexiest, funniest man I've ever met". He was born
Michael Micklewhite in Bermondsey, London in 1933,
son of a fish porter and a charwoman. When he emerged
in "Zulu" in 1963 he had put in 10 hard years playing
repertory and small film roles. Once a star, he went along
with his Casanova image, squiring a succession of beauties, but then settled down near Windsor with his Moslem
wife, Shakira Baksh. He has a teenage daughter by a
previous marriage.

Casanova's contemporary portraits do less than justice
to his charms. Giacomo Girolamo Casanova
(1725-1798), an Italian adventurer left an imperishable
myth of Latin sexual stamina in his autobiography,
"Histoire de ma Vie". Born in Venice and rapidly expelled
from a seminary after "scandalous" conduct, he began
wandering the capitals of Europe, turning his hand to
religion, music, writing, gambling, diplomacy, finance
and even magic – a crime for which in 1755 he was sent
to prison for five years, shortening this with a dashing
escape from the Doge's Palace in 1756. After a duelling
scandal forced him to flee to Spain, he returned to Venice
as a spy for the Inquisition. He ended his days in peaceful
pursuit of the women of Bohemia.

Judging by his own account (and the indignation of
many cuckolded contemporaries) his ardour, his reputation, his wit and his dark looks invariably overcame the
resistance of women of all ages, classes and situations.
An Italian writer, Dr Luigi Barzini, has pointed out that
Casanova's psychological endurance was even more
remarkable than his virility. He retained, throughout
innumerable affairs, a schoolboyish eagerness. Like the
English writer, Frank Harris, who bragged of similar
exploits in a more recent autobiography, his claims can
never be proved. But unquenchable desire is an attractive
fantasy and Casanova's legend is secure.

*Casanova, said one writer, had the capacity to satisfy
"the most exacting mistress by renewing his homages
to her a practically unlimited number of times".*

David Cassidy, who has made a career of looking dewy-eyed. His stand-in on television's "The Partridge Family" was a girl. His cuddly attraction appeals to thousands of teenage girls around the world.

D avid Cassidy, a musical throwback to the Prince Charming tradition, is, with Donny Osmond, the most cuddly of today's screamybopper heart-throbs. Though older than he looks (his birth-date is usually given as 1950, in New York), he represents to thousands of teenage and sub-teenage girls, the ideal of an eternal sexual childhood in which relationships with boys will be soft, sweet-smelling and non-frightening. His manager, Ruth Aarons, comes close to the mark when she says he "really represents happiness".

She discovered her "super-puppy" in 1968 when his father, Jack Cassidy, a minor actor, told her his son was interested in the stage. After appearing in a short-lived Broadway musical, he auditioned successfully for a string of television serials, culminating in his 1970 appearance in a new series "The Partridge Family". As the sparkling-eyed 16-year-old son of Shirley Jones (who is his real-life step-mother), he soon began to dominate the show. Music for the rock-and-roll Partridge band was dubbed by off-camera musicians, but to everyone's delight, David revealed that he could sing as well as act. With the release of "I Think I Love You", which sold 5 million discs he became a concert superstar, first in the U.S. and then in Britain. Slight, (5ft 8in), with brown hair, hazel eyes and a perfectly-shaped dazzling smile, he projects a dewy innocence as yet undimmed by the hysteria of his fans who, when he appears in public, barely pause to remove their David Cassidy bubble-gum before shrieking in unison. David himself keeps his starry distance, prefers the company of his room-mate, Sam Hyman, admits to one unhappy affair, likes playing the piano, admires Paul McCartney and does nothing to spoil an image as wholesome as an apple.

Bonny Prince Charlie's recent biographers have not been kind to him. Charles Edward Louis Philip Casimir Stuart (1720-1788), grandson of the exiled James II, in 1745 attempted to drive the Hanoverians off the English throne and re-establish a Catholic monarchy. His callow optimism and pig-headed pride led directly to the savage destruction of the Highland clans after the enterprise ended in failure at the battle of Culloden in April, 1746. The Young Pretender nevertheless remains the most glamorous underdog in history. The pretty-featured, flaxen-haired 25-year-old who landed with seven men on the West Coast of Scotland had enough charm and daring to lead the Highland army as far south as Derby before the nerve of his generals failed and they turned back to Scotland (seeing no English enthusiasm for Charles). To their dismay, the Prince who had been so magnanimous and confident in victory, became sulky and apathetic in defeat. But five months wandering in the heather consolidated the appeal of the Bonny Prince, carried "over the sea to Skye" by brave Flora Macdonald and to eventual safety in France.

Nobody remembers that the Young Pretender actually paid a secret visit to London in 1750, that he married an obscure princess (Louise of Stolberg) at the age of 52 and that his last years were marked by drunkenness and fear of assassination. The bare bones of his story are less important than what he stood for – passionate loyalty to a lost cause, defiance of the weight of numbers and the romance of a successful escape. If Charles Stuart had not existed, Scotland would have had to invent him to carry a minority people's poignant burden of poetry, story and song.

An engraving made from Sir W.W. Wynne's picture of Bonny Prince Charlie, the Young Chevalier. His personal attraction won over many Scots sceptical of his cause.

Montgomery Clift, leader of a blank-stare style of introverted acting which poignantly expressed in films the tension of a post-war generation.

Montgomery Clift was the answer to the need of postwar youth for a hero who would face bleak realities with a new sort of disillusioned courage. They were able to identify with this dark, wiry actor with a stubborn jaw and deep-set eyes, who came across as a sensitive outsider, hunched in his shell like a wistful crab. Clift's first film, "Red River" (1948) pitted him against a pig-headed Western strongman, played by John Wayne. Clift lost the fist-fight but won the hearts of a generation which identified with his coolness, his will to survive and his contempt for brute force. To the traditional attractions of outward male courage, Clift added a fashionably-neurotic air of inner conflict. In "A Place in the Sun" (1951) he portrayed a youth corrupted by middle-class values. The silent perplexed gaze which now became his dominant acting trick was imitated everywhere. A year later, he reached the high point of his film career when he played Prewitt, the inflexible loner of "From Here to Eternity" who said: "If a man don't go his own way, he's nothin'."

The attitude was close to Clift's own personality. Born in 1920 in the U.S.A. into a well-off Omaha family, he had gone his own way almost from the age of 15, when he began working on Broadway as a child star before playing leading stage roles with the Lunts. He was a prickly, hard-drinking, easily-offended individualist who insisted on a rare degree of independence when he arrived in Hollywood in 1947. His capacity to handle his personal problems was impaired by a near-fatal car accident in the mid-1950s. This damaged his facial muscles and in his later films his gift of compressing emotion tended to turn into a stark-eyed blankness. By the time of his death, at 45, his career was in decline. He was essentially a youth hero – together with Marlon Brando, probably the most influential male actor of his own generation.

S̶ean Connery, in his interpretation of James Bond, has (see page 16) managed to change the character to his own image so successfully that Ian Fleming said, ''He is Bond as I envisaged him.'' Which is a tribute to Connery's acting ability, because he is not much like the cold, suave character of the books. Connery has been called a dour, uncouth, tight-fisted, bad-tempered Scot. On the other hand, his former wife, Diane Cilento, who married him in 1963, described him as docile and patient. Either way, he is certainly a warmer personality than Bond, whom he always played with his tongue firmly in his cheek.

Born in 1930, he was the son of an Edinburgh truck driver. He left school at 15, took a succession of jobs on a milk round, in the navy, as a swimming pool guard, as a bricklayer and as a coffin polisher, and developed a build which won him a small role in the London run of ''South Pacific'' in 1951. He modelled swimming trunks,

In his determination to be his own man, Sean Connery is more conscious than most actors of being identified with the character he is playing. He once said women would ''run a mile'' if he began behaving like James Bond.

got some repertory and television experience in the 1950s and was picked in 1963 for what was expected to be a modest B-grade sort of film, ''Dr No''. Instead it was a hit, and the next two Bond films put Connery among the biggest money-earning stars in cinema history. An informal, beer-drinking, football-loving type (he has ''Scotland Forever'' tattooed on his right arm), Connery got fed up with publicity which identified him with Bond. Since 1967 he has turned down big offers in favour of screen and stage work which show a wider range and power. If he manages to shrug off the super-virile Bond image completely, women will probably still mob him. With his huge shoulders, furrowed cheeks and large, gentle eyes, Connery radiates male strength and energy in the same way that Clark Gable once did.

Gary Cooper brought chivalry with him when he rode into town. A kind of cowboy Sir Galahad, he embodied the traditional virtues of the Western hero – courage, sincerity, integrity and unfailing courtesy toward women. His 6ft 3in of lean, blue-eyed handsomeness, his quiet humour and his "yup, nope" conversational style created a legend of courtliness that Americans almost began to believe existed in that never-never frontier land where "Coop" wore the sheriff's badge and always got the girl. Frank James Cooper (the Gary was suggested in 1926 by an agent who came from that town in Indiana) came to California in 1924 hoping to sell political cartoons. When he couldn't, he took work as a cowboy extra, having learnt stunt-riding on his father's farm in Montana where he was born in 1901. He had been to school in England and college in Iowa but had also spent a lot of time on the ranch convalescing from a car accident which fractured his hip and left him with his distinctive, rolling, bow-legged gait.

He began his 36-year career as a star with "The Winning of Barbara Worth" in 1926, carried on a rather

The mature Gary Cooper, grim-faced as he stands alone at the climax of "High Noon", the 1966 film which won him his second Oscar. He personified an American ideal – the man of few words and unswerving courage.

self-conscious series of romances with Clara Bow, Evelyn Brent, the Mexican ''spitfire'', Lupe Velez and Countess Dorothy di Frasso, and then married Veronica Balfe in 1932 – a marriage interrupted only by a brief separation in 1951. Soon after playing a bashful millionaire in ''Mr Deeds Goes to Town'' (1935), he became one. He won six Academy Award nominations, two Oscars (for ''Sergeant York'' in 1941 and ''High Noon'' in 1952) and a special award not long before he died of cancer in 1961. The poet Carl Sandburg called him ''one of the most beloved illiterates this country has ever known''. Cooper was a naturally conservative and taciturn man who, by playing himself both on and off the screen, created an enduring legend. His appeal to women was a mixture of shy niceness and protective manliness and the combination never became outmoded.

El Cordobes' world is the bullfight which has always been heavy with sexual symbolism. The horned bull is male, the exhibitionist finery of the matador, female. But as the matador's sword penetrates the bull's neck, the image is suddenly reversed. Since the late 1950s, Spain has had a bullfighter who has added to this already dramatic spectacle, his own unusual personal magnetism. Manuel Benites (El Cordobes) has become not only the idol of the Spanish masses but also one of the highest-

El Cordobes, the daring and reckless matador. Of women, he told one interviewer, ''They're beautiful even when they are ugly''. Of marriage, though, he said it leaves a man ''no longer free to die''.

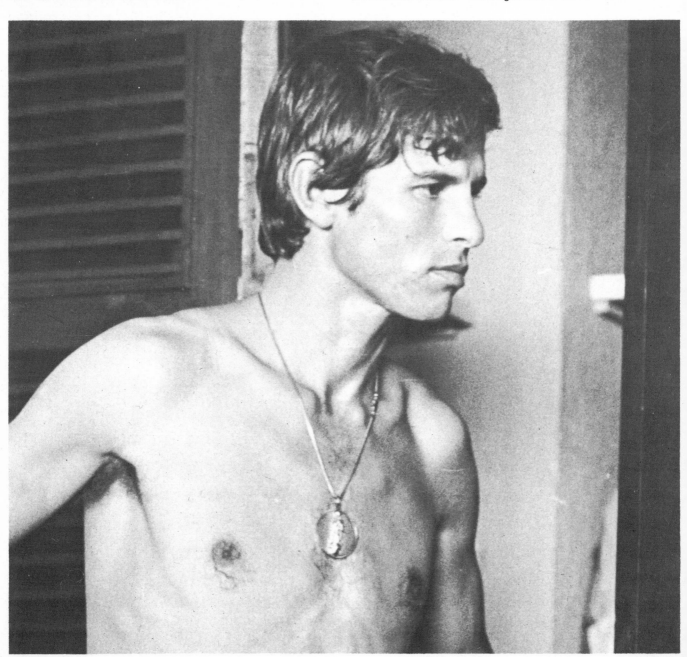

paid entertainers in the world, earning nearly £1 million a year at the peak of his career. By 1967, when he briefly retired after seeing visions of death, he had killed a thousand bulls and survived 11 gorings. Worse was to come in 1968 when a rival jumped into the ring and waltzed with the bull he was fighting. El Cordobes' henchmen were said to be snipping the horn tips and sand-bagging the necks of bulls he was scheduled to meet. But despite all his showmanship, El Cordobes has been the most reckless matador in the history of the game, as the scars on his lean body testify.

Born in an Andalusian slum in 1935 and orphaned at 9, he was still an illiterate roadworker in 1956 when he jumped the barrier at a corrida and showed off some passes he had practised on a ranch by moonlight. He was tossed out of the ring. At 24, he got another chance and began to astonish crowds with his suicidal courage, kneeling and skipping around the bulls making dazzling linked passes and flashing ''the fastest teeth in Spain'' at the ladies. To his delirious followers, he is the greatest of all bullfighters. To others, he is a flamboyant clown. Nobody disputes his animal sexuality though. Under a boyish mop of coarse brown hair, the swarthy skin is stretched over a broad, chunky face. The eyes are sharp as a bird's, the walk is strutting, aggressively masculine.

El Cordobes is now looking after a successful business empire and has even announced vague plans to marry Martine Rayasse, the French mother of his two children. But he shows no inclination to give up his other role as free agent, escort of princesses and actresses, favourite of Franco and latterly, candidate for film stardom (when he has learned more English). El Cordobes is living proof that danger is still one of the most powerful aphrodisiacs of all.

David, the Biblical shepherd boy who slew Goliath with a sling-shot is most accurately depicted in a statue by Bernini. He stands in a Rome museum, drawing a bead on his target with the shrewd, calculating eye of a skinny young athlete. But the heart-throb David is Michelangelo's – a statue of overwhelming power around whose stone masculinity, busloads of female tourists forever circle with fluttering hearts. (The lucky gallery is the Accademia in Florence.) If David looked like this, how big was Goliath?

Michelangelo's famous marble David, a statue measuring almost 13½ feet high, was started in 1501 and completed in 1504. It now stands in the Accademia di Belle Arti in Florence. The attraction of the biblical David comes from a combination of adherence to principle and basic aims and flexible and shrewd political action. Michelangelo's rendering of David captures a mood of strong physical capacity together with a feeling of sensuality and classic balance.

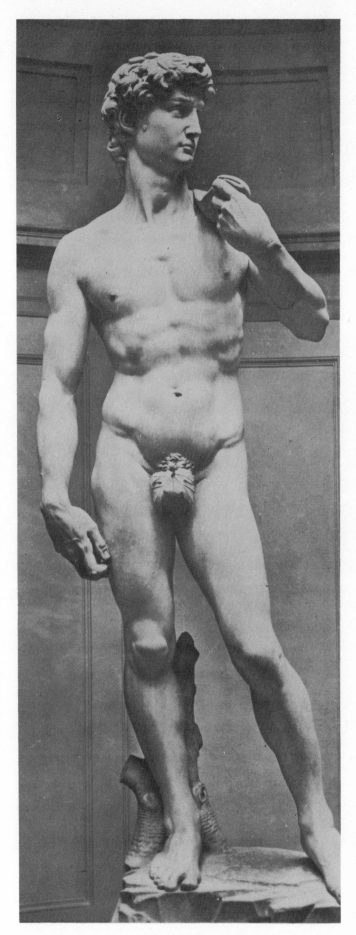

James Dean was the best-known victim of the generation gap. "The only greatness is in immortality", he said not long before he was killed in a sports car crash. Against the odds, he has achieved immortality in the memory of his own post-war generation – and a more ghoulish fascination for followers of the personality cult that sprang up when he died in September 1955. His reputation as a symbol of disillusioned youth rests on only three films, two of them released after his death. Such secure fame could only have been achieved through a remarkable public identification between Dean himself and the film roles he played.

He was born in Fairmont, Indiana, in February, 1931 and might have been a conventional middle-class American youth had his mother not died when he was nine. He was brought up by an uncle and aunt and when he left school to join his father in California found he could not communicate with him. He dropped out of both law school and an arts degree course at The University of California and after a few jobs as a film extra, went to the Actor's Studio in New York. Elia Kazan picked him for Steinbeck's "East of Eden" when Marlon Brando was unavailable. When the film came out many critics felt Dean's performance was modelled on the Brando proto-type of the rebel. In fact, he was much closer to the shrinking style of another contemporary, Montgomery Clift.

Dean did not have Brando's frightening physical power. Lean, blond, with rather defenceless blue eyes (he wore glasses), a nervous, unaccountable smile and prematurely creased face, he looked like an all-American boy with a bad streak. In "East of Eden" he projected restless energy and a baffled, inexpressible need to be loved. His off-stage liking for liquor and speed, the impression of a haunted headlong rush towards destruction, was confirmed by his death at 24. "Rebel Without a Cause" was issued a month later on a wave of adolescent self-pity. Spiritualists claimed he was keeping in touch with them; ghouls chipped fragments from his grave; some of his fans still hoard his personal things as souvenirs.

The wistful, longing element in his makeup was carefully shielded by his wild behaviour, his scruffy blue jeans and sneakers, his facial grimaces and surly manner. As his last film, "Giant", showed, he was a considerable actor. But it was his own disturbed personality, projected by directors who understood his affinity with the emerging anti-materialism of American youth in the mid-1950s, which gave him his place as a non-conformist hero to both sexes.

Left *James Dean in "Rebel without a Cause", the film that began a Dean cult and an enthusiastic following when it was released after his death in 1955.*

Below *A scene from the film "East of Eden", based on the John Steinbeck novel, in which James Dean plays a sensitive young man from the Southern states.*

Kirk Douglas is a blue-eyed blonde with a dimpled chin. But his eyes seem to be roasting and his jaw looks as if it is crushing stones. Only James Cagney acted with as much driving intensity. As a heart-throb, Douglas forces his way in through sheer aggressive egotism. When columnist Sheila Graham heard he would play the lead in ''Young Man With a Horn'' in 1950, she said it would be a cinch because he never stopped blowing it. His name used to be Issur Danielovitch Demsky. He was born in New York in 1916 of Russian refugee parents, was an inter-collegiate wrestling champion and did some professional wrestling while studying acting. After navy service and stage and radio work, he did well opposite Barbara Stanwyck in a 1946 film and was chosen to play the ruthless pug in ''Champion'' (1949). His specialities ever since have been muscular hero-heel roles or parts calling for the ferocious temperament he displayed so effectively in ''Lust for Life'' (1956). A serious and intelligent actor in the right films (''Paths of Glory'' was the best), Kirk Douglas interests himself in art, languages and politics and entertains stylishly in Hollywood with his French second wife whom he married in 1954.

Blonde, blue-eyed Kirk Douglas as he appeared in ''Is Paris Burning?'' in 1966. He is sometimes mistaken for that other screen heart-throb, Burt Lancaster.

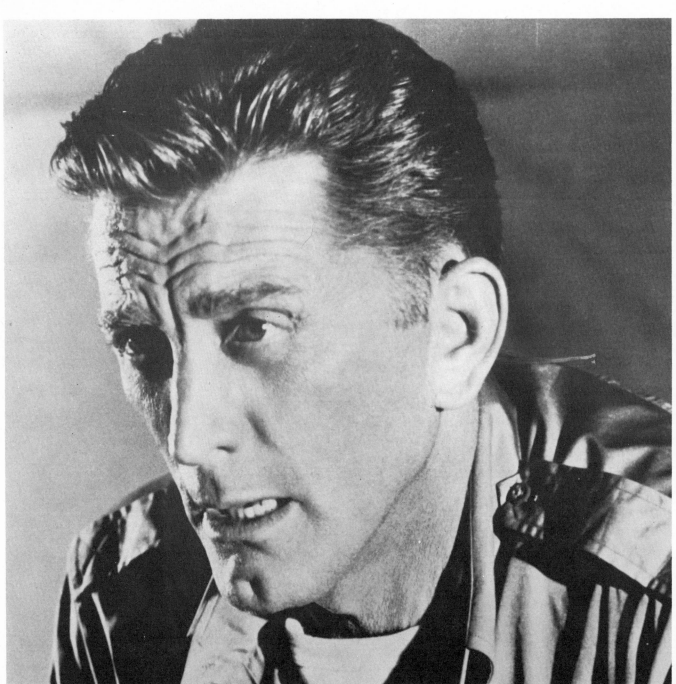

Clint Eastwood, the latest and coldest of a long line of Western heroes. Usually cast as a silent, violent figure in a black sombrero, he has a tightly-drawn, pale face which gives nothing away.

Clint Eastwood's parts in the "spaghetti Westerns" of Italian director Sergio Leone have made him one of the top-drawing stars in the world. But he is probably the most colourless sex hero in cinema history. Usually cast as a silent, violent figure in a black sombrero, he has a tightly-drawn face which gives nothing away and kills with a detached brutality. He is a San Francisco accountant's son, born in 1933, and was an athletics coach when he met his wife Maggie and began picking up small film and television parts in the 1950s. In 1959, he began a long run as the lead in television's "Rawhide". But it was only when Leone chose him for "The Man With No Name" that he began to be a name. He directed a classy thriller "Play Misty for Me" in 1971 and has continued to refine his own image as the cool, ruthless outsider without quite convincing critics that his appeal is distinct from the box-office violence of most of his films. Leone chose him for his quality of stillness, the force of screen presence in his lean 6ft 4in frame and his pale, calm face. To his critics, he is the embodiment of computer sex. But one of his co-stars, Susan Clark, believes the impression he gives of lonely self-sufficiency is the basis of his attraction: "Part of his sex appeal is the constant mystery: How deeply does he feel? How deeply is he involved in life?"

Douglas Fairbanks – "He smiles and you feel relieved", wrote the film critic Alistair Cooke. "At a difficult period in American history, Douglas Fairbanks appeared to know all the answers." Today, the name of Fairbanks is associated with the tradition of swash-buckling flamboyance carried on by his son, Douglas Fairbanks Jnr, in costume romances of the 1930s and 1940s. But this was not the secret of the elder Fairbanks' hold on the imagination of the American public. He appeared on the screen in 1914, just as the world was drifting into the first fully-mechanized war. The technological age was about to overtake the old-style hero who relied on simple strength and courage to protect his women from harm. For a few heady years, the zest, optimism and acrobatic energy of Douglas Fairbanks preserved the illusion that these qualities were still the answer to most problems.

His real name was Julius Ulman. He was born in 1883, son of a Denver lawyer, and had a fairly conventional middle-class upbringing with a spell at Harvard, as a businessman, and as a young-man-about-Europe, before trying the stage. In 1914, D.W. Griffiths decided he had the right brown-eyed, breezy charm for a series of short silent films based on sophisticated satires of American life by Anita Loos. By 1917, Fairbanks was famous. He was a kind of plainclothes Superman, jumping, swinging or vaulting over obstacles with casual grace. In a typical scene in "The Matrimaniac" he overcomes the lack of a phone by simply walking along a telephone wire and asking a surprised linesman to plug him into the number he wants. In 1920, he married the "nation's sweetheart", Mary Pickford and with Griffiths and Chaplin they formed United Artists. Fairbanks became the apostle of non-smoking, non-drinking joy through strength. To his Hollywood gymnasium came all the sporting, diplomatic and political heroes of the day for instruction on the virtues of outdoor life. He identified himself so thoroughly with Good Causes that his popularity survived even the shock of his divorce from Mary Pickford in 1928.

But his earlier nonchalant charm evaporated as he began to make ever-more lavish costume spectaculars. Acrobatics gave way to muscle building and to stunts which tended towards self-parody. They were not always as effective as the delightful sequence in "The Black Pirate" (1926) in which he appeared to slide down the huge sail of a galleon with only his dagger slitting the canvas as a counterweight. After 1934, he left the screen to his more debonair son. The irony of his death in 1939 was that his over-developed burliness may have contributed to the circulatory trouble that killed him.

Douglas Fairbanks smoking a rare cigarette in "The Mark of Zorro" – in the 1920s he became the apostle of non-smoking, non-drinking joy through strength.

Albert Finney's sensation performance in the 1960 film "Saturday Night and Sunday Morning" made it inevitable that he would be typecast as a "British Brando". He was the first postwar British actor to project the kind of aggressive virility that had made Brando famous 10 years earlier. But Finney, with his broad, tough, boxer's face and disarming grin was a more down-to-earth sex symbol than the 1950s had seen. The North Country dialect, the thirst for beer, the over-boisterous lust, the blunt humour and the stubborn courage of the character he played opposite Rachel Roberts gave the screen an authentic working-class hero straight off the factory floor, brimming with a mixture of vitality and discontent. Finney's reputation as a womaniser (at least on the screen) grew with "Tom Jones" in 1963, an unexpectedly successful film in which his own freshness and vigour won him critical awards at Venice and New York – and made him a millionaire.

He was born in 1936 in Salford, Lancashire, where father was a bookmaker. After acting in school plays he won a scholarship to the Royal Academy of Dramatic Art and went on to the Birmingham Rep. where Charles Laughton saw him and was deeply impressed. Finney continues to be fascinated by the stage, returned to it for the National Theatre in 1965-66 and is still a dominant force in British drama. An explosive temper (he once told an audience he would go home if they didn't shut up) has not prevented him becoming a self-effacing director, as he showed in his sardonic 1967 film, "Charlie Bubbles". His early marriage to a student actress broke up in 1961 and he married Anouk Aimee in 1970.

Albert Finney – tough, aggressive, virile – burst into notice in 1960 with his sensational performance in the film, "Saturday Night and Sunday Morning".

Errol Flynn spent most of his adult life looking like the fictional character at whom irate fathers are always shouting "You impudent young scoundrel" and with whom their daughters are always eloping. His air of injured innocence, his clipped English voice, his astonishingly handsome features and the imperturbability with which he faced bullet, sword or rope in a 20-year career of screen adventure made him the Walter Mitty hero of all time. The imperturbability wasn't feigned. Flynn was 6ft 1in, well-built, and knew how to use his fists. David Niven, who was acting with him in the 1936 version of "The Charge of the Light Brigade" recalls how a beefy stunt rider on the set of the film mistook Flynn's insufferably heroic air for mere play-acting. As the brigade lined up with Flynn in front, the stuntman leaned forward and prodded his horse in the rear. Flynn was thrown flat on his back, dusted himself off, told the stuntman to dismount and belted him. The stuntman did not repeat his action.

Flynn's reputation as the playboy of the Western world landed him in more serious trouble. In 1942 a girl he had met at a party on a boat brought a charge of statutory rape against him. Though the case was clearly trumped-up and he was acquitted, there were columns of court evidence and some of the dirt stuck – particularly when another publicity-seeking girl brought a similar charge (also dismissed) eight years later. Even the young companion of his last years, Barbara Aadland, was to sue his estate for "corruption of morals". With prophetic resignation, Flynn had said after his last film: "The rest of my life will be devoted to women and litigation". He had no regrets about his hard-living image. "The public has always expected me to be a playboy and a decent chap never lets his public down. I'll live this half of my life. I don't care about the other half." And Flynn did live up to his playboy image.

The half he lived began in 1909 at Hobart, Australia, where his Irish father was working as a professor of marine biology. Flynn was kicked out of private schools there and in Britain and claimed to have got his real education as a ship's cook, a boxer, a reporter, a pearl

Dashing swordplay from Errol Flynn in the 1940 film, "The Sea Hawk". He preferred to duel with stuntmen rather than actors who might get carried away, especially after Anthony Quinn nearly ran him through!

diver and a colonial officer in New Guinea. His first contact with film work was as a guide with a 1932 expedition to the interior of New Guinea led by Dr H. Erbin who was making a documentary. He was in two British films before Warners spotted him in 1934. On the boat to Hollywood he met and married Lili Damita, an actress with whom he had a son, Sean, and some spectacular public feuds before their divorce in 1942.

Flynn's dashing swordplay in ''Captain Blood'' (1935) cast him in a cardboard hero mould from which he could never quite escape. He was tried in several comedy romances opposite actresses like Bette Davis but did not look as if he was taking it seriously enough. Eventually, he resigned himself to soft leather boots and string-tied jerkins, the screen world of Sherwood forest, ship's riggings and castle battlements and to the legend that he could not act. ''I don't want to say all that old boy'', he is supposed to have said to one director. ''Just give me a quick line to read.''

Errol Flynn – the playboy of the Western world – was an unlikely Soames in this 1950 version of ''The Forsyte Saga''. The film was a lack-lustre affair and Flynn's own career was soon to enter a decline.

During his 1942 trial he met his second wife, Nora Eddington, who was a cigarette girl at the courthouse. ''He wasn't afraid of anything, particularly if there was a challenge to it'', she was to say later. They had two children and he had another daughter with his third wife, Patrice Wymore, his co-star in ''Rocky Mountain'' (1950). Alimony, taxation and maintenance debts, together with the bottle, began to get the better of him in the 1950s. He left Hollywood in 1952, sought sanctuary on his yacht and at his Jamaican estate, ''Castle Comfort'', and tried his hand at independent production without much success. After a surprisingly good performance in ''The Sun Also Rises'' (1957) he went adventuring again in Cuba and produced a series of articles called ''I Fought With Castro''. He had already published two books and a third, his wry autobiography ''My Wicked, Wicked Ways'' appeared posthumously. He died in 1959 in Vancouver where he was trying to sell his yacht, leaving the taxmen and his former wives to fight over an estate of $2.6 million. Flynn's charm lay in his combination of wildness and mildness. ''For the life of me'', he once said, ''I can't understand why a quiet, reserved fellow like me should be involved in the news so much.''

Henry Fonda in the 1957 film classic, "Twelve Angry Men". Fonda's performance in this famous film, as a juror who refused to be stampeded by emotion, won him a British Film Academy Award.

enry and Peter Fonda project two images of the American Way of Life. Since Peter emerged as a youth hero in the mid-1960s, the styles as father and son have also provided a fascinating contrast between two generations of heart-throbs. They share the lanky limbs, the grave facial expression, the wide, fringed eyes, the quiet, almost toneless voice. But whereas the father has always stood for idealistic democracy, the son has become the symbol of youthful pessimism.

Henry Jaynes Fonda is a Nebraskan (born 1905). He came to Hollywood after a long stage apprenticeship which began in Omaha where he started out as a physical education coach. He emerged as the voice of rural integrity in John Ford's ''The Grapes of Wrath'' in 1940.

'This great film was both a protest against social injustice and an affirmation that the people could change society. On the screen, Fonda projects a surface calmness which hides a coiled spring. The gentle eyes can suddenly freeze, the dusty voice turn hard as steel. He is that most enduring of Early American heroes, the man who stands up to the mob and lets the light of reason into a prejudiced court-room or a tyrannized community. Off-screen, ''Hank'' Fonda is an active Democrat, a rather reticent and serious gentleman and, since 1965, the husband of a former air hostess 27 years younger than

Peter Fonda as Captain America in his own production, with Dennis Hopper, of "Easy Rider" – the parable of the loss of individual freedom in America which made him a cult hero of the young, and a millionaire.

himself. The mother of his famous children, Peter and Jane, was Frances Brokaw, who committed suicide in a mental clinic. Fonda has been married five times. Of his own marital disasters Fonda has said he "loved them all and could not have saved one of them".

Nor, apparently, could he save Peter from growing up a disillusioned rebel who blamed his father for his troubled adolescence. Peter was born in New York in 1939, was shifted around a series of private schools and expelled from one at 16 for punching a teacher. (He had earlier wounded himself with a gun on hearing of his

mother's suicide.) He married Susan Brewer in 1961, had two children and tried clean-cut roles on the stage and in films during the early 60s without much success. But his non-conformist image was given a boost by widely-publicised experiments with drugs, including an arrest in 1966, and by his association with American International which produced "The Wild Angels" the same year. A brutal "bikie" movie, this was the forerunner of other films in which he played anti-authority roles, culminating in his shoestring 1969 production of "Easy Rider" which made him a millionaire by grossing over $20 million. As Captain America who "blew it", Peter Fonda became a fully-fledged cult anti-hero. His sceptical message for the 1970s was that the search for freedom is doomed to failure and that the "cool" thing is to recognize that the odds are stacked against liberty.

Jean Gabin, the remarkably durable hero of the French cinema was born in 1904 and was still France's most popular actor in 1970. Owner of the most stoical face in film history, he began as a kind of Bogartian tough and in his later performances as the famous Maigret, progressed towards a shrewdness and solidity reminiscent of Spencer Tracy. His real name was Jean-Alexis Moncorge. His parents were in vaudeville and he began his own show business career in revues after working as a builder's labourer. He married Gaby Basset, first of his three wives, in 1928 and began to build up a reputation during the 1930s in films of Renoir, Duvivier and Carne. "Pepe le Moko" (1937) gave him an international audience, though he was never to make a successful transition to Hollywood. His forte was the victim-hero – a man trapped by fate, resigned to an imminent punishment and offering to his admirers only the comfort of his own courage. In films like "Le Jour Se Lève" (1939), he caught the authentic mood of pre-war France and gave a romantic colouring to the despair of a whole nation.

Jean Gabin, a star of the French cinema since the 1930s when he emerged from cabaret to play the film roles that made him an existentialist hero of wartime France.

Clark Gable was the one they sent for whenever Hollywood wanted a he-man. His imposing shoulders, tom-cat grin, bunched eyebrows and abrupt voice dominated the screen so completely and over such a long period (30 years) that if any male star had to be singled out as the greatest sex symbol of them all, it would probably be him. They began calling him "the King" in the 1930s after his co-star and rival, Spencer Tracy, irritably presented him with a brass crown because a crowd of Gable fans had blocked Tracy's way into the MGM studios. The joke was that Gable was about the least aristocratic man imaginable. In the sex comedies of the early 1930s it was Gable who first levelled social barriers by telling uppity ladies where to get off. He was the hero of an era in American history when the old class-conscious morality was being swept away along with many of the economic privileges of the Establishment. When Gable slapped Norma Shearer's face in "A Free Soul" and told her: "You're mine, and I want you", the genteel lovers of the day began to look effete.

"It was Gable who made villains popular", Norma Shearer said. By 1939 when the American public was asked who should play Rhett Butler, the ruthless hero of the best-selling novel "Gone With The Wind", nobody could see past him. The role not only kept Gable in front of the public with successive releases of the film. It also established his legend as a super-virile, mockingly-confident male, contemptuous of moral hypocrisy and female prudery; in one scene, Scarlett O'Hara (Vivien Leigh) was shown waking and stretching happily in the rumpled bed upon which Gable had thrown her during a blazing row the night before.

The apostle of brute masculinity was born in Cadiz, Ohio, in 1901. His mother died only weeks later and his father, a dour oil-rigger, was hard on young Billy (Clark was his middle name). He was too husky and slow-witted to be comfortable at school and though he hit it off with his step-mother there was nothing to hold him after she, too, died before he was out of his teens. He moved around Oklahoma and Oregon as a mechanic, oil-rigger and lumberjack but was gradually becoming fixed on the idea of a stage career as a means of escape from manual labour. His bumbling crudeness brought him a good deal of ridicule. The manager of a stock company who auditioned him said he had nothing to offer as an actor. But his potential as a rough diamond was recognized by a drama coach, Josephine Dillon, who married him in 1924 (she was 14 years older) and worked hard to put some polish on his brawny frame. By the late 1920s his country-boy gaucheness was disappearing, he began

The legendary Clark Gable with Jean Harlow in 1937 in "Saratoga". Harlow was his favourite leading lady for her ability to take it and dish it out like a man.

getting Broadway roles and he was taken in hand by a wealthy Houston socialite, Ria Langham, whom he married in 1931.

The same year, MGM decided to overlook his big ears (Howard Hughes said they made him look like a taxicab with both doors open) and put him into a succession of quick films. His impact on women audiences was electrifying. By 1935, when he won an Oscar for ''It Happened One Night'' with Claudette Colbert, he was the fantasy lover of every shop-girl in America, and of a good

Clark Gable's performance as the breezy reporter of ''It Happened One Night'', with Claudette Colbert, won him an unexpected Academy Award as Best Actor in 1935.

many of their upper-class customers as well. In spite of his male chauvinist screen image, Gable's ideal woman was the sort who could hit back with a man-to-man toughness. He found her in Carole Lombard, with whom he had a zestful, prankish love affair which began in 1936. They married in 1939 and were inseparable until

1941 when she went on a bond-selling tour. The plane in which she was returning to Los Angeles hit a peak between Nevada and Death Valley during a snowstorm and there were no survivors.

Gable, then 41, finished the film he was making ("Somewhere I'll Find You"), joined the Army Air Corps and spent much of the war in Britain where he flew bomber missions over Germany shooting a training film for gunners. Postwar life without Carole Lombard tested his powers of survival in a Hollywood where the big-star system was crumbling under the impact of television. But despite some indifferent films, the old aura of dark, cocksure power remained. He weathered well enough to go on playing romantic roles throughout the 1950s. A 1949 marriage to Lady Sylvia Ashley was short-lived – she tried to feminise the hunting-shooting-fishing atmosphere of the Gable ranch at Encino. But in 1955 he began a happy marriage to Kay Spreckles, who looked uncannily like Carole Lombard.

In 1960, when shooting finished on "The Misfits", Gable was looking forward to the birth of his first child. But the film, shot in desert temperatures of over 100° Farenheit overtaxed his strength. His co-star, Marilyn Monroe, was in a neurotic state which caused endless filming delays and Gable's frustration led him to attempt physical feats a man of 59 should have left to a stuntman. Four days after filming ended he had a heart attack from which he never recovered. Ironically, "The Misfits" was a failure. Gable had hoped it would sum up his whole acting career. Its prophetic theme was the decline of the mystique of simple outdoor virility under the pressures of urban materialism. The era of the simple he-man star Gable had personified for so many years was also passing. Joan Crawford, one of his co-stars, said he could always come into a room and make every woman in it aware of him before they had turned their heads to look. Gable's father's contempt for the acting profession did leave its mark on him in a self-conscious insistence that all his screen roles should be "manly" in the corniest sense of the word. But both on and off the screen his sheer physical presence was overwhelming and his self-assurance was genuine and without vanity.

In the 1930s, Gable had been well ahead of his time as a screen hero. His impudent attitude to authority, his grudging chivalry and his frankly amoral approach to sex was more typical of the anti-heroic postwar actors. But the missing element in Gable's appeal to a later generation was his absence of complexity and self-doubt. The personality he projected in nearly all his films was supremely confident. He looked as if he could take on anything with his bare fists – office bosses, gangsters, wild animals or women. "I'm no actor and I never have been", he said. "What people see on the screen is me. The only reason they come to see me is that I know life is great and they know I know it." Admirable though the Gable attitude was, it might not have convinced the sceptical world of the 1960s.

Sir Galahad of Arthurian legend represents the ultimate dream of chaste maidenhood – a man who will serve them to the death without thought of selfish gain (particularly sexual gain). In Sir Thomas Malory's *Morte D'Arthur*, Galahad is the son of Sir Launcelot. But unlike his father, who is led astray by his sensual appetites and becomes the lover of Queen Guinevere, he is a youth of unassailable purity. He is able to wrench from a block of red marble a sword which can be withdrawn only by "the best knight in the world". Thus armed, he defeats seven knights, rescues countless maidens from captivity and eventually finds the Holy Grail – the dish of the Last Supper. Having looked on its radiance, the virgin knight is carried to Heaven. It is sadly difficult to think of a less fashionable contemporary hero.

Sir Galahad, the original knight in shining armour, was a Victorian pin-up but in the 20th century, heroes are usually of more assailable purity.

John Garfield was the forerunner of a male type that was to dominate the screen from the mid-1950s – angry, alienated and cynical, a radical change from the debonair or uncomplicated heroes he followed. He was a dark, nuggety actor with heavy, furrowed brows, a square cleft chin and the look of a boyishly undamaged boxer. Garfield was born Julius Garfinkel on New York's East Side in 1913. His mother died when he was seven and his father, a coat-presser, remarried and moved to the Bronx. The boy was drifting into petty thieving with a gang of juvenile thugs when a child psychologist took an interest in him and sent him to drama school to correct a stammer. By 1937, he was playing leads with the left-wing Group Theatre. His childhood sweetheart, Roberta Seidman, supported him by clerical work until he became established.

It all sounded like a script for one of his own films. True to the scenario, his personal life began to go awry after he arrived in Hollywood in 1938. He and his wife separated when his name was linked with Hedy Lamarr and they were reconciled only in 1945 when their daughter died during a picnic (apparently from choking). In 1950, his socialist beliefs brought him to the attention of the House Committee on Un-American Activities and he disappointed many of his friends by denying any communist links. By then an influential actor-director, he was nevertheless suspended from film-making pending an FBI investigation. He prepared but never finished a statement putting his political beliefs into perspective. At 39, he suffered a fatal heart attack in New York in the bedroom of an ex-actress. There was a wave of public remorse and *Newsweek* reported the biggest display of grief for a film star since the death of Valentino.

The novelty of Garfield's screen image is clear from reviews of his first film "Four Daughters". The *New York Times* said Micky Borden, the out-of-work musician he played, was "a sweet relief from conventional screen types". He is a wry, sardonic, chain-smoking fatalist who shocks a small town with his anti-social opinions and surly behaviour, marries one of the town's good girls, then decides he is no husband for her and manages to get himself killed. In many of his 30 films, this kind of role became stereotyped. Garfield was Warner's "official gall and wormwood taster". His toughness and realism was nevertheless attractive to a generation of women whose men had to battle their way out of a Depression and through a war. "What can you do, kill me?" the boxer hero of "Body and Soul" asked the mobsters who wanted him to throw the fight. "Everybody dies."

The rise of John Garfield was a striking example of the connexion between screen heroes and the needs of society. A boy from the wrong side of the tracks, he gave a generation of Americans, dispossessed by the Depression, an authentic voice of bitterness

John Gilbert was America's first homegrown Great Lover. By an accident of timing, he was also the last of the screen heroes whose romantic appeal was grounded wholly in fantasy. Because he tried to leap the gap between silent films and the greater realism of the talkies, he suffered the indignity of becoming laughable. Audiences are said to have tittered because his voice turned out to be unexpectedly high. More probably, Gilbert was let down by a failure to adapt his acting style. Silent films called for an exaggerated pantomime of passion which had to be toned down once it was put to words.

What made Gilbert so successful in the 1920s was that he was a genuine romantic to whom exaggeration came naturally. He was an ingenuous, boyishly temperamental man who acted best when he was carried away by his own feelings. With Greta Garbo this led to an electric give-and-take which made their 1927 film "Flesh and the Devil" a sensation. Researchers reported that college students experienced a kind of erotic osmosis as they watched the love scenes, imagining themselves literally in Gilbert's arms. Apart from the music there was nothing to interrupt the dream. Aside from a slightly bulbous nose (which he grew his dapper moustache to counterbalance) Gilbert had all the physical attributes the dream required – dark brown hair curling above a broad forehead, lustrous brown eyes with flashing whites, an aggressive jaw and a piratical grin.

He was born John Pringle in 1897, son of an actor-manager. Though he was appearing in films from 1917 onward he initially wanted to be a director and began playing romantic leads only after a directing fiasco. His success amazed him and he began to believe in himself as the personification of the male lover, extending his film characterizations into his private life with almost absurd enthusiasm. He gave his yachts names like "The Witch" and "The Temptress" and would order Russian balalaika players and caviare for his parties to complement his on-screen role as a cossack. He believed so passionately in his own dashing image that he took it as an affront to his virility when critics and audiences made fun of his first talking pictures in the early 1930s. Though his tenor voice was no worse than some others, it did not match the high-flown screenplay. He began drinking, left his first wife to marry Virginia Bruce and developed a paranoid hatred of Louis B. Mayer and of the studio which had been quick to turn against him once he lost his public. In 1934 he appeared once more with Garbo, whom he had pursued ardently for two years in the 1920s. His last part was as a sarcastic drunkard – a role close to the man he had become. Like Garfield, he died of a heart attack at 39. The Hollywood dream machine was never quite the same again. A man whose romantic appeal had arisen out of silent films had died and with him a memorable era.

illy Graham's image works. "We are selling the greatest product on earth", say his campaigners. "Why not package it properly?" Dr Graham's sex appeal is an undeniable part of the package, as hundreds of women suddenly smitten by religion at the Graham crusades could bear witness. He is tall, lean, flat-hipped, with an out-thrust jaw and wavy fair hair. His eyes look like blue fibreglass in a tanned face. Though he is in his mid-50s, he seems shiny new. On the platform, his voice and his jabbing finger are urgent and commanding; off it, he is relaxed, smiling, courteous and humble. His message is one of hope, even joy, and it is delivered in simple terms that contain never a hint of ambiguity or doubt. To anyone tired of life's complexities, a decision for Christ and Billy Graham must come as a tremendous relief. Many people are drawn to his crusade meetings and many people find a great deal of comfort – both physical and mental – from his religious message.

The gospel superstar was born in 1919, son of a farmer in Charlotte, North Carolina, where he still lives with his wife and five children. After being impressed as a youth by a travelling evangelist, he enrolled at 18 in a Bible institute in Florida, wrestled with his conscience there and finally made his personal decision for Christ (on his knees at the 18th green of the college golf course). He learned something about salesmanship selling brushes from door-to-door in the Depression, took an anthropology degree at Bob Jones University, Illinois, married the daughter of a missionary in 1943 and became a pastor in the Southern Baptist Church. But it was when he joined Youth for Christ that his ability to sway crowds emerged. After preaching to thousands in a tent in Los Angeles in 1949 he became a national figure and set up his own non-profit evangelist business. Donations to the work of his mission average about £3 million a year.

His impact as an evangelist is carefully stage-managed. Crusade meetings are orchestrated to produce successive moods of worry, fear, tension, unity, obedience, climaxed by the emotional release of his own offer of salvation. But Dr Graham's glamour is based on more than his aura of power and success. He is a throwback to the male conventions of an earlier era – straight and strong, big and handsome, clean-cut and gracious, optimistic and sincere. The type has its attraction still.

Left *John Gilbert – a genuine romantic to whom exaggeration came naturally and America's first homegrown Great Lover. Such were his exuberance and good looks that he almost melted the heart of the great Snow Queen, Greta Garbo.*
Right *Straight and strong, big and handsome, clean-cut and sincere, Billy Graham's glamour is a throw back to the male conventions of an earlier era.*

Stewart Granger's qualities that once made him unpopular off the screen were the same as those that made him, with James Mason, the British cinema's only glamour-boy of the 1940s. He projected a male arrogance which, according to one woman admirer, made her feel she was "drowning". This was in part the result of his natural cockiness and in part created by close-set eyes which looked down the Granger nose in apparent disdain. The effect was magnificently aristocratic.

He was born James Stewart in London in 1913, went to drama school and had some stage and film experience before the war. Invalided out of the Black Watch in 1942, he built his reputation as a romantic star mainly on a series of Gainsborough films, beginning with "The Man in Grey" in 1943 and ending with his move to Hollywood in 1950. He married Jean Simmons the same year and was later to claim that he had played in poor films to support her in better ones. Whatever the reason, his roles became increasingly shallow and he was unable to switch to character acting; with typical outspoken humour he said his fate was to go on looking like "an old leading man". During the 1960s he played in several European films, went ranching in Arizona and had two more marriages.

Cary Grant, born Archibald Alexander Leach was nearly 30 when Mae West saw him walking across a film lot and said: "If he can talk, I'll take him." That was in 1933. Hollywood renamed him Cary Grant (partly to annoy Gary Cooper with whom the studio was having trouble at the time). As the years went by, the debonair 6ft 2in British actor with the cleft chin, dark brown eyes and neat hair got better and better looking until nobody could remember his age. "How old Cary Grant?" wired a publicist who needed to know. And according to the Hollywood legend, Grant saw the cable and cheerily answered: "Old Cary Grant fine. How you?" It is an anecdote with all the buoyant charm that has been the essence of Cary Grant's style. Once George Cukor began directing him in 1935, he became the most skilful romantic comedian in the business and the man, one columnist said, "every woman over 25 has dreamed of loving". His appeal was based on an inimitable clipped voice and a combination of size and lightness, masculinity and grace.

His deftness was the legacy of an early appren-

Left *Stewart Granger, British cinema's only glamour-boy of the 1940s, in a 1952 version of "The Prisoner of Zenda", made soon after he left for Hollywood.*
Right *Cary Grant, famed for his debonair good looks, infectious optimism and impeccable comic style, is one of the best actors never to have won an Academy Award.*

ticeship as a mime artist, acrobat and stilt-walker. He was born in Bristol, England in 1904, lost his mother when he was 10 and at 13 ran away to join a pantomime troupe in Brighton as a refuge from an unhappy school life. Though he was returned to the classroom, he rejoined the troupe as soon as he could and spent five years learning the vaudeville trade, arriving in New York with the company in 1922. He stayed on, working a Coney Island concession and turning his hand to everything from painting ties to mind-reading. Then came musical comedies in Britain and on Broadway and his arrival in Hollywood in 1932.

He played the Salvation Army captain to whom Mae West (as a saloon-keeper) said: "Why don't you come up sometime and see me?" in the 1933 comedy "She Done Him Wrong". Most of his screen career from then on was spent in casual but calculated pursuit of women. His films were based usually on the delightful fantasy that the problems of life can be reduced to a series of romantic misunderstandings. Off-screen misunderstandings involved him in a series of marriages, at least one of which was fondly remembered — by his second wife, Betty Hutton, who countered stories of his legendary stinginess by saying that he was the only husband who did not take a dime from her. His fourth wife, Dyan Cannon, whom he courted for four years in the 1960s, said in her divorce suit that he was mixed-up. "When I'm married I want to be single and when I'm single I want to be married", he told a columnist. Since the mid-1960s Grant has put his gregarious and likeable personality to work as a businessman involved in air transport and cosmetics.

The Guevara student posters that declare "Che Lives" claim no more than the truth. Ernesto "Che" Guevara had become a legend even before his lonely death at the hands of a drunken Bolivian sergeant. The years since 1967 have only consolidated his place as the most fashionable left-wing hero of the 1960s. To teenagers who know nothing of his revolutionary ideas the face on the photographs has its own emblematic sexual power — the dark, long-lashed eyes, the curling hair and beard, the jutting cigar, the black cap. The image is reinforced by the environment in which he lived — the jungled mysteries of Latin America which are as exotic to the urbanized West as Sherwood Forest might have been to the townspeople of medieval England. Then there are the dramatic contrasts of his life: The asthmatic child who became a leader of astonishing endurance; the qualified doctor who became a guerilla fighter; the Government Minister who renounced power in his middle age to become a hunted fugitive; the sensitive poet who became

Che Guevara as Cuba's Minister of Industry. Renouncing power to become a fugitive in the Bolivian jungle, he became a legend in his lifetime.

a man of violence.

Guevara was born in Argentina in 1928, took a medical degree and then travelled widely in South America, working at a variety of jobs. The poverty and political corruption he saw in the early 1950s made a deep impression on him. As a 24-year-old in Guatemala, he watched the CIA-backed overthrow of the Popular Front Government of Arbenz Guzman which both confirmed his anti-Americanism and convinced him that revolutions are fought with "bullets, not peaceful protests". He met Fidel Castro in Mexico and joined him as the party's doctor when Castro launched his daring expedition into Batista's Cuba in December 1956. The 15 men who reached the safety of the Sierra Maestra became the nucleus of a peasant army which eventually defeated Batista's 25,000 troops.

Guevara, who had become ideologist, tactician and second lieutenant of the Cuban revolution, never seemed as happy wielding power as he had been winning it. He was put in charge of Cuban education, then industry. He published in 1960, a classic book on guerilla warfare. But he had what Castro called a "Garibaldian dream" of freeing the whole of the Latin American continent. Suddenly he disappeared from Cuba. There were reports of him in the Congo, Santo Domingo, Vietnam. Early in 1967 it became known that he had entered Bolivia the previous November with 17 Cubans and placed himself at the head of a small Bolivian guerilla force. He hoped to repeat the Cuban miracle in an area of Bolivia close enough to the borders of Argentina and Peru to draw these countries into the revolutionary struggle. But the environment was inhospitable. The local Indians were, he said, "impenetrable as rocks". The Bolivian troops hunting him were more effective than he had expected. And there is some evidence that the Bolivian Communist Party let him down.

The strangest part of the Bolivian adventure was the ambiguous role played by a dark, handsome East German woman named Tamara Bunke (known to Guevara as Tania), who joined him in the hills and was killed in an ambush shortly before he himself was trapped. She had been sent to Cuba by the KGB to spy on Guevara, whose policies both as Cuban Minister of Trade and later as an agitator, conflicted with some aspects of Soviet policy in Latin America. Tamara was the fourth important woman in Guevara's life. He had loved an Argentinian aristocrat whom he left when she would not follow him into Marxism, his first wife, Hilda Gadea, a Peruvian communist, and his second wife, Aleida.

A month later, Guevara himself was wounded in the thigh when a patrol of Bolivian Rangers caught his dwindling band in a ravine. His carbine was shot out of his hands and he was taken as the army's prisoner to a nearby village. The next morning October 9, 1967, he was summarily executed. His hands were cut off for finger-printing and his body burned and buried in a secret grave. The legend, however, could not be killed.

Richard Harris admitted a few years ago that the image most people had of him was of a mad Irishman running along a beach with a bottle in his hand. His reputation for hell-raising, his gingery granite face with its much-broken beak of a nose, the residual memory of his wide-shouldered 6ft 3in frame crashing upfield in the Rugby League film that made him famous, "This Sporting Life" (1963), all contributed to an impression of dumb brutishness. This is not, however, what gives Harris his present romantic vogue. It is the breathy baritone ballads of records like "A Tramp Shining" and the image of his blue-eyed King Arthur, sadly reflecting on lost love upon the battlements of Camelot. He has been able to express through his film and singing career, his personal progress from youthful brawling to the recognition that violence is self-defeating.

Irish – born in Limerick, Eire, in 1933, educated at a Jesuit college and at the London School of Music and Dramatic Art, he moved into films in the late 1950s after working with Joan Littlewood's experimental theatre. He had celebrated squalls with Charlton Heston, Kirk Douglas and Marlon Brando, who sulked when Harris reacted to some unconvincing punches on the set of "Mutiny on the Bounty" by kissing him on both cheeks and inviting him to dance..Harris' off-screen career as "the Mixer" was never the same after 1967 when his wife (mother of his three sons and daughter of Liberal peer Lord Ogmore) left him. He played King Arthur in "Camelot" the same year, began singing gentle ballads and eventually made a remarkably successful tour of America with a programme of sentimental songs and poems. To impressed teenagers in the audience, he seemed "human, not a showbiz phoney". The giant had a tender heart.

Richard Harris with Vanessa Redgrave in "Camelot". His gentle King Arthur – a sexual loser – was a change from a more brutal and rumbustious image.

eathcliffe, the brooding hero of *Wuthering Heights* is the archetype of a long line of thrillingly frightening lovers in women's fiction. Authors of less power than Emily Bronte, who wrote *Wuthering Heights* in 1847, have trivialized her idea of a passion that lasted beyond the grave. But the figure of Heathcliffe is recognizable behind all those dark, mysterious, violent and tortured heroes who crowd the pages of magazine stories and light romantic novels. Heathcliffe was a gipsy orphan brought into the lonely Yorkshire household of the Earnshaws, where he is loved by Catherine Earnshaw and treated badly by her elder brother. When the children grow up, Catherine decides to make a conventional marriage with a rich neighbour, Edgar Linton, who is a genteel contrast to the surly stableboy Heathcliffe has become. Heathcliffe disappears for some years, returns from South America, rich and bitter, possessed by a combination of passionate love for Catherine, and an undying desire for revenge.

Catherine, unable to live through this, falls fatally ill and on her death-bed the pair confess their love in an agony of remorse.

Looked at objectively, Heathcliffe is a sado-maniac. But *Wuthering Heights* was the apotheosis of the romantic concept of love as an obsession which sweeps aside norms of behaviour. ''He's always in my mind'', says Catherine, ''not as a pleasure, any more than I am a pleasure to myself, but as my own being''. The morose, implacable lover with ''depressed brows and eyes full of black fire'' was superbly played by Laurence Olivier in a 1939 film version. Heathcliffe was the product of Victorian sexual repressions and of Emily Bronte's own life with her autocratic father and tormented brother. Except as a figure of melodrama, he may not survive the advance of sexual equality.

Heathcliffe, the brooding hero of ''Wuthering Heights'', played by Laurence Olivier, in William Wyler's film version of the famous Bronte novel. Merle Oberon was Cathy.

Charlton Heston's roles in films vary widely from Moses in "The Ten Commandments" to the circus manager in "The Greatest Show on Earth". Some claim that his "head prefect" image has hampered his success, but his many fans would disagree with this.

Charlton Heston, if Hollywood is to be believed, not only looks like Michelangelo but like General Gordon and Buffalo Bill as well. No actor has had greatness thrust upon him so often. And none illustrates more intriguingly the difference between a hero and a heart-throb. Though Heston ranks second only to John Wayne at the box office, he has surprisingly little romantic charisma. Perhaps his aquiline handsomeness is too obvious. Perhaps the roles he plays are too forbidding. Or perhaps it is just that he looks too virtuous to be much fun. Sex and spectacle do not seem to mix and though Heston always looks convincing, his acting lacks that latent power which generates tension and identifies star presence.

A quiet, thoughtful and conscientious man, Heston tells a nice story about how Cecil B.De Mille picked him to play the circus manager in "The Greatest Show On Earth" (1952) because "he liked the way I waved". De Mille was also struck by Heston's resemblance to the Michelangelo statue of Moses and it was the role of Moses in "The Ten Commandments" (1956) which really established him as Hollywood's resident saint and hero. Heston himself says his greatest asset is his commanding nose (broken in a football accident). He was born in Evanstown, Illinois, in 1923, majored in drama at North-Western University and did stage radio and television work before going into films. He has been married since 1944.

Dustin Hoffman in ''Little Big Man''. He first emerged as a heart-throb in his comic role in ''The Graduate'' as the young man pursued by the renowned Mrs Robinson.

Dustin Hoffman needed more than an average share of luck to make him a heart-throb. A single film, ''The Graduate'', lifted him from obscurity to the cover of *Time* magazine and to the focus of a whole generation's rebellion against American materialism. Mike Nichols, who directed the film, deliberately picked an anonymous face for the purpose. It was not the usual stuff of romantic dreams – sleepy brown eyes, a longish nose, a small mouth and a slightly undershot jaw. But its very averageness concentrated its charm for youthful audiences who saw Hoffman walking in a kind of trauma away from a postgraduate world of plastics, escaping the cynical arms of Mrs Robinson and finally snatching her daughter from the altar and rejecting the distorted values of adult society. A more conventional screen hero would have looked less convincing.

Hoffman's subsequent films have shown he is no ordinary actor however. Son of a Los Angeles furniture designer, he was born in 1937, studied medicine and then switched to acting. He had already begun to make an impression off Broadway when Nichols noticed him. In 1969, he married Anne Byrne, a former dancer, and has concentrated on living a private life. He worries about the personality pressures of being a ''star'', points to the tragic example of James Dean who let the public turn him into a myth and has sought self-knowledge through psycho-analysis. Hoffman's wary pessimism and his complexity come through in his screen performances and make him an authentic non-hero to his own alienated generation.

Robin Hood, as he is seen by tourists in a statue at Nottingham, the traditional locale of his exploits, where he robbed from the rich to give to the poor. He is thought to have lived in the 13th or 14th century.

Robin Hood, feared by the bad, loved by the good, is the most durable English heart-throb of them all. He is relatively sexless by contemporary standards. His relationship with Maid Marion runs more to chivalry than to reckless passion. But he has masses of dash, charm and insouciant courage and is one of the earliest rebel heroes. As a scourge of rich, fat, greedy monks, the Robin Hood of legend is a composite figure based on many medieval tales and ballads. There is no historical basis for the most popular story that he was the rightful Earl of Huntingdon, forced to live on his wits by the skullduggery of King John and the Sheriff of Nottingham. But it is certain that tyranny and misused power did drive many well-born men outside the law and that some of them became folk heroes by helping the needy with the proceeds of what they took from the rich.

The two earliest histories to mention Robin, place him in the reign of either Henry III (when he could have been a follower of Simon de Montfort in the revolt of 1264) or of Edward I. Records do show that a certain Robert Hood lost land during the reign of Edward II, whose household he later joined in 1324. This would tie in with the story that Robin received a kingly pardon in return for his services. Maid Marion is a much later addition to the story. Her appearance reflects the growing romantic appeal of Robin Hood – forerunner of a male type that was to come into its own once the 20th Century swept away the social rules that put outlaws out of bounds as lovers.

Rock Hudson exudes a kind of self-effacing likeability; and some unkind wit once said he had plenty to be modest about. To an extent, Hudson was the victim of an era of blatant commercialism in Hollywood which turned him into a teeth-capped "Baron of Beefcake" during the early 1950s before he had learned to act. Tall, big-shouldered and brown-eyed, he based his appeal largely on a combination of solidity and gentleness and on a boyishly-winning smile. He came across as a kind of hulking, soft-hearted truck driver.

Roy Fitzgerald, from Illinois (born 1925) had in fact worked as a truck driver and also a vacuum cleaner salesman and a postman, before he was befriended by an agent (whose secretary he later married and divorced) and was given a small part in "Fighter Squadron" (1948). By 1952 he was starring in mediocre action films, but it was not until his performances in "Giant" and "Something of Value" (1957) that he began to have a large following. His sex comedy series with Doris Day, beginning with "Pillow Talk" in 1959, kept him near the top at the box office until 1965. By then the star system which had made him was at its last gasp and audiences have since turned to less glossy pin-ups.

The Rock Hudson smile at full flow in "Pillow Talk", first of a highly successful comedy series with Doris Day. Hudson tried to break out of his Hollywood mould of handsome he-man in the 1966 film, "Seconds".

ick Jagger emerged just when Western society thought it could leave primitive phallus worship to the research of anthropologists. He is the most aggressive symbol of male eroticism in the history of entertainment, the high priest of a pop cult based on musically-amplified jolts of raw sexual power. When the Rolling Stones emerged from the suburban London club where they were playing in 1963 and began casting offensive matter at their elders, nobody expected them to last. They seemed a musically-ordinary bunch of shaggy primitives whose imitation of Negro rhythm-and-blues would not survive once the Establishment grew tired of scolding them. But as the years went by and their musical showmanship improved, the magnetism of their lead singer, Mick Jagger, increased. He seemed able to sustain the anger of the Stones' initial revolt against authority and even to accelerate it.

The surprising thing is that off the concert platform, Jagger does not come across as an angry personality at all. He has no particular reason to be. Michael Philip Jagger, born 1943, is the son of conservative parents with whom he had a friendly, if distant, relationship. His father taught physical education at a training college in Dartford, where Jagger won a scholarship to grammar school and, apart from wearing his hair long, was a normal, successful student. Since he gave up his studies at the London School of Economics in 1963 to form the ''Stones'' with rhythm guitarist Keith Richard, he has never had to struggle for success. In one year alone, the ''Stones'' sold 10 million singles, 5 million LPs and £2 million worth of concert tickets.

Jagger's use of ''pot'' (he has never advocated hard drugs) brought him a brief jail sentence in 1966 and the status of a marijuana martyr. But otherwise he has seldom been harassed by authority and his life-style is not dramatically unconventional. After two long and stormy

Below *Jagger became a rebel for what he was, not for what he believed. He represented the ''ugly idol'', the other end of the spectrum from the smooth matinee idol.*

Right *The dark and dynamic Mick Jagger in concert, ''looking'', said one critic, ''for all the world like a bird of paradise hurling himself about the stage''.*

relationships (with Chrissie Shrimpton and Marianne Faithful) he even got married and he and Bianca have a small daughter. He is not politically committed to rebellion, is slightly-built and rather unassertive, and according to his mother, is also rather insecure and lonely. His stage personality, however, is startlingly different. The Rolling Stones saw when they started out that the basic drive of the Negro rhythm-and-blues bands was racial resentment. For this, they substituted a resentment against society's perpetual wish to tame, tidy and quieten its youth. They glorified noise, dirt and a kind of uncouth gracelessness. They were right in thinking this image would simultaneously arouse the fear and anger of parents and a corresponding sympathy among many teenagers. And they have moved along ever since on a tide of adult annoyance and active hatred.

The most potent weapon with which they could batter the over-30s was sex. Instead of keeping it away from young people and allowing adults to go on controlling, curbing and guiding adolescents, Jagger and the Rolling Stones set out to unleash their sexual emotions. In his stage shows, Jagger uses the full range of stimulants – rhythm, words, lights, costumes, make-up and movement – to generate a wave of sensual excitement on which he rides. The comparison with the mating rites of the animal kingdom and the phallus worship of primitive societies is irresistible. Decked out in peacock finery with his face painted and his chest bared, Jagger struts and prances, jerks and swings in a frenzy of male arrogance, creating what he himself calls a ''dialogue of energy'' with the mass hysteria of his audience. The music itself often appeals directly to adolescent frustrations (''I Can't Get No Satisfaction'') and Jagger's combination of masculine power and feminine grace, his pelvic gyrations, his taunts and shouts, are all part of a parade of sexuality as self-conscious as the choreography of a ballet. Jagger used to think he was ugly. But his gaunt face with its canine eyes and rubbery lips is an essential part of the strange appeal of the Rolling Stones. They set out to frighten society and it is Jagger who most of all supplies the daemonic element.

Tom Jones, a totally masculine tease who can sing 'I Need a Woman' and look as if he meant it. He was the first Welsh singer to conquer American night clubs.

om Jones is a far cry from the old tradition that male singers were not supposed to flirt with the audience too openly. They could do a bit of elegant hoofing, tilting their top hats, twirling their canes and even blowing kisses. But strip-tease was left to the ladies. Not any more. The best example of changing attitudes to what a male performer can do while still remaining clearly male is Tom Jones, the pride of Pontypridd, Wales. He was born there in June, 1940, Thomas Jones Woodward. By the age of 16 he was using his big shoulders to heave bricks and his big baritone voice to sing in local Welsh clubs. His first record, ''It's Not Unusual'' was a smash hit, projecting him into a concert, nightclub and television career which reached a peak at Las Vegas in 1968 when Frank Sinatra modestly introduced him as ''the greatest''.

Like Sinatra himself, Jones is a master of lyric phrasing, imposing his individual style on all his songs. But it is showmanship that has made him a pin-up, his anguished ''come-on'' techniques which provoke women of all ages to scramble on stage for kisses or fight for the jacket he throws into the audience. His black hair tossing in glistening curls, his ringed hands, his brawny torso, his lean hips swinging suggestively in skin-tight pants, all proclaim the liberated male who is sure enough of his own virility to be able to decorate himself enticingly – and even have his nose bobbed – without losing the old aura of sweat and brickdust. Jones has managed with some success to reconcile the wealth and glitter of showbiz with his beer-drinking, dart-playing family origins. When he is not working, he retreats to Weybridge, Surrey, where he lives with his wife, Linda, their teenage son, and his parents next door.

Louis Jourdan said, ''It is assumed that a good-looking man is also an imbecile. Many handsome men never mature. They always remain boys.'' It sounds like a sad self-epitaph to his film career. A quiet, introspective and intelligent actor, he was unable to escape from the stereotyped young lover roles in which he was cast as ''the handsomest Frenchman alive'' during the 1950s. He was born Louis Gendre in Marseilles and worked on the French stage and in films after leaving drama school in Paris. He was already 28 when he arrived in America in 1947. But Hollywood saw him purely as a juvenile lead. Films like ''The Swan'' (1956) and ''Gigi'' (1958) exploited his 6ft elegance, his thick black hair and warm brown eyes, his fetching accent and his earnest attentiveness to women.

Louis Jourdan, at his well-groomed best in ''Gigi'', the 1958 musical based on a story of Colette's which won eight Oscars for production but none for its stars. Jourdan was built up from the Hollywood machine.

Don Juan, the fictional counterpart of the real-life Casanova, is usually identified as a young nobleman of Seville who dedicates himself to the unscrupulous pursuit of women. In Byron's long satiric poem, he is sent abroad at the age of 16 and wanders the world in search of amorous adventure. But the most romantic version of the legend is Mozart's "Don Giovanni". In the true spirit of modern heroism, the profligate Don refuses to repent as the gates of Hell yawn and chooses to die with his principles intact.

Don Juan in amorous dalliance in an 18th century engraving. The fictional counterpart of the real-life Casanova, his name has become the synonym for lechery.

Kennedy, the family name, is a legend of 20th century America. John Fitzgerald Kennedy (1917-1963) had a glamour quite different from that which usually attaches itself to a young man who becomes a political leader. His brother Bobby inherited and even heightened the political charisma of the Kennedy name. But the magnetism of John, and to some extent of Senator Edward Kennedy, seems to be separate from their political careers and inherent in their personalities.

Physically, John Kennedy was a warm, sandy man with a bush of chestnut hair, ruminative eyes and a lanky, high-shouldered frame that made him look vulnerable, even when he filled out from being a gangling Senator and became President. His shy, earnest quality was combined with an abrupt, urgent voice and an impression of vitality and determination which reminded Americans that they were dealing not with a bumbling, ingenuous young candidate such as James Stewart might have played on the films, but with the millionaire son of Joe Kennedy, a Boston-Irish businessman of legendary toughness.

The steel beneath John Kennedy's "ordinary" exterior was first shown when, after graduating with honours from Harvard and writing a book on pre-war English attitudes, he served in the Navy. His PT boat was rammed in the Solomons and he received a back injury which was to plague him for the rest of his life. But he was able to tow another injured sailor three miles, gripping the strap of his life-belt in his teeth. When a schoolboy asked him years later what it took to become a hero he said: "It was easy – they sank my boat."

The mixture of dedication and self-deprecating wit was the essence of the Kennedy style as America perceived it when the young ex-Congressman (1947-53) and Senator fronted up to the television cameras in the historic series of debates which helped him to defeat Richard Nixon for the Presidency in 1960. "Grace under pressure" became the hallmark of the Kennedy Administration. JFK and Jackie (whom he had married in 1953) and their children represented the idea that the nation could be led by a man who could meet great challenges without losing touch with young people, without becoming dull and humourless and without growing cynical. Events since Kennedy's assassination in Dallas on November 22, 1963 have only deepened the nostalgia with which Americans look back at a man adored as perhaps no other political figure has ever been adored.

The appeal of his youngest brother, Teddy, is mixed inextricably with this nostalgia. But the fact that he can still be seen as a strong contender for the Presidency, even after Chappaquiddick, suggests that he must have

"Of those to whom much is given, much is required" – though born to wealth, John F. Kennedy sought challenges and became a popular political figure.

something more than the potency of the Kennedy name going for him. To women, his most obvious asset is his looks. The tall, impeccably-dressed frame, the keen blue eyes, the big white teeth and aggressive jaw, the broad chest with its mat of hair, all give an impression of strength. In a curious way, Teddy is therefore the reverse of John. For where John combined moral strength with a good deal of ill-health, Teddy has combined physical strength with moral failures at crucial points of his career.

Born in 1932, the ninth child of Joe and Rose Kennedy, though he has now inherited leadership of the clan, he somehow remains the kid brother. As a boy he was sunny-tempered and gregarious. At Harvard, his casual approach to study led to an expulsion for cheating. He was readmitted in 1953, after military service, completed an honours degree and scored a touchdown

Still overshadowed by his two brothers, John and Robert, Edward, perhaps the best-looking of the Kennedy brothers, hopes to equal their fame and achievements.

against Yale, married a pretty blonde, Joan Bennett in his last year at law school and has been in politics since 1957. He is physically daring and was accident-prone even before the Chappaquiddick incident when he panicked after crashing off a bridge and for some hours failed to report the drowning of the girl he had been driving. Since that traumatic experience he has rehabilitated himself with some hard work in the Senate. To the American people, Teddy has some of the charm of the prodigal son. It is as if they hoped the Kennedy story could after all have a happy ending; that a confessed backslider could turn into a hero like his brothers.

Jean-Claude Killy was mobbed by flower-throwing girls after he had hurtled down the slopes of Grenoble to win three Olympic gold medals for skiing in 1968. He is the best Alpine racer in the history of the sport, and the man who skied, as the French say, "casse-cou" (breakneck). He is also good-looking in a square-cut, furrowed way – 6ft and 170 lbs of lean muscle with keen blue eyes and shaggy brown hair. Apart from the strength of his legs, which rode the bumps of downhill courses like steel springs, the distinctive mark of his racing style was guts. Arms flailing, skis parting, he looked, and was, on the brink of disaster. "I take all the risks", he said.

Killy was born in St Cloud, Paris, in 1943, son of a former fighter-pilot who moved to Val D'Isere to run a hotel there. To Jean-Claude, skiing became like breathing. He dropped out of school at 15, took a job as a Customs officer which allowed him to ski constantly, was French junior champion by 1960 and world champion of 1967. Though he is now a successful business-man, speed remains an obsession. He is a racing driver of near-professional standard. Killy's appeal is a compound of athleticism, modest self-confidence, courage and identification with skiing – the most glamorous sport of them all. The mystique of the mountains – sunburned faces, white teeth and apres-ski romance in fetching knitwear – can make almost any ski instructor seem like a hero. Killy is the ski instructor nonpareil.

Henry Kissinger made a marvellous centre-fold in the Harvard students' "send up" of the magazine *Cosmopolitan*. He knows his appeal. "Power", he said, "is the greatest aphrodisiac". A superb public relations operator, Dr Kissinger has almost managed to persuade women that he is a heart-throb as well as a formidable statesman. His owlish, rotund figure has been seen at the side of some of the most beautiful women in America. Dr Kissinger, who has been divorced for some years and has a teenage son and daughter, can be a lively and charming companion. But one French journalist who tried to have a more lasting relationship with him than casual dates at social functions, had to confess that his mind was on other things.

Jean-Claude Killy finished yards ahead of his competitors in a sport of speed and skill in which victory is usually measured in fractions of a second.

America's Secretary of State, Dr Henry Kissinger. Once a long-standing bachelor, he recently married Nancy Maginnes, his steadiest woman friend.

Burt Lancaster in his 1956 "Trapeze" where he played a not-so-young high flier who had been crippled in a fall but returns to the big top as a catcher.

Burt Lancaster once terrorized a Hollywood producer by standing on one hand on a 10in ledge outside his third-storey office, muscles bulging and white teeth bared in an upside-down grin. His teeth and muscles, his blue eyes and wavy fair hair, have always made him a physically overwhelming actor, but Lancaster has been shrewd enough to escape being typecast purely as an aggressive he-man and has based much of his appeal to women on a controlled gentleness, an ox-like pacifism.

Still super-fit at 60 (he was born in New York in 1913), he is an ex-circus acrobat who graduated from jobs as a postal employee and floorwalker to stage experience as an actor and dancer in an army entertainment group. His first film, "The Killers" in 1946 (he played the indomitable ex-pug of Hemingway's story) was outstanding. And though his acting is often flawed by a too-conscious charm, he has continued to be a formidable performer, winning an Oscar in 1960 for "Elmer Gantry" but giving his best in "The Rose Tattoo" (1955). Lancaster's 1946 marriage lasted 23 years and produced five children. He is a natural leader (Hecht-Lancaster was the first actor-controlled production company in the postwar period) and was a vigorous fund-raiser for social causes and civil rights. But he was once known for his cocksureness and a black temper. It may be this contradiction in his personality which gives his screen presence its power – the impression of anger under tight control.

Charles Lindbergh rode high on a revolution in transport, communications and the mass media during the 1920s which made him the most idolized figure of his day after he flew the Atlantic single-handed in 1927. To a public fed on tabloid newspaper sensation, he seemed to represent shining idealism, courage and adventurousness in an age of cheap heroics and tawdry triumphs. Part of his attraction came from being the first man to accomplish a feat never done before. His solo flight displayed bravery, tenacity and physical endurance – qualities which most women find appealing.

Lindbergh was 25 when he set off in his monoplane, the Spirit of St Louis, to fly the 3600 miles to Le Bourget, France. He had been born in Detroit and had been flying since 1921 as a stuntman, joyride pilot, instructor and mailman. When a $25,000 prize was offered for the Atlantic flight, he persuaded a group of St Louis businessmen to back him in building a plane which he stripped to the bare essentials. Even then, the plane was so loaded with gasoline that it barely cleared trees and wires on takeoff. Others had already died trying to make the crossing. Brown and Alcock, who actually flew the Atlantic first in 1919, had crashed in an Irish bog. Lindbergh himself had to fly without wireless, steering by map and stars and struggling to stay awake against drowsiness and bitter cold during his 33½-hour crossing.

Newspapers and the radio extracted every ounce of drama from the suspense. A huge crowd in the Place de l'Opera roared as illuminated messages announced that ''Lindy'' was over Ireland, then England, and finally that he had landed at Le Bourget at 10.30 p.m. on May 21. ''Well, I'm here'', he drawled. ''Are there any mechanics about?'' Blond, open-faced and gawky in a borrowed brown suit, he posed for photographers, looking chokingly boyish. The adulation he received on both sides of the Atlantic, but particularly in America, was incomparably greater than anything that would later be given to the more technical triumphs of the first men on the moon. It was poignantly heightened in 1932 when the son of his marriage to Anne Spencer Morrow was kidnapped and found murdered after a ransom had been paid.

Lindbergh, by then an Air Force colonel, went on to become a successful businessman and a passionate spokesman for American isolationism at the beginning of World War II. Though he could still generate mass hysteria among women who heard him speak at Madison Square, his reluctance to condemn Naziism tarnished the image that made him, in the words of one writer in 1927, ''a modern Galahad for a generation which had forsworn Galahads''.

Charles Lindbergh, hero of an era when the men who flew planes still seemed more important than machinery or computers. This photograph was taken after ''The Spirit of St Louis'' made its historic crossing of the Atlantic.

L‌awrence of Arabia, (T.E. Lawrence, 1888-1935) was a figure of almost unreal romance during his lifetime and the years since his death have embellished his legend to the point at which he is in danger of becoming a heart-throb in spite of himself. The photographic bravura of David Lean's 1963 film about him has already converted ''T.E.''s slight 5ft 8in figure, his weather-beaten face with its long, solemn jaw, broad upper lip and bristle of hair into the devastatingly handsome image of Peter O'Toole

Lawrence of Arabia dressed for the sands of the desert – a romantic image that stirred the imagination of two generations of Englishmen – and women. He died in a motor-cycle accident in the mid-1930s.

– 6ft 2in, violet-eyed, silky-haired, brooding gracefully in the folds of a snow-white turban.

Lawrence's brother, a professor, barely recognized the real man when he saw the film. It showed a rebellious British officer who escaped from the tedium of army life to lead the Arab uprising of 1916 against their Turkish masters, enlisted the aid of Bedouin irregulars to attack Aqaba and harry the Turkish army, but saw his poetic dream of a united Arab State dissolve in bickering after the successful march on Damascus which ended the desert campaign. Though heightening his personal heroism, the film followed the details of Lawrence's army career closely enough. What Professor Lawrence objected to was its interpretation of Lawrence's character – not only that he was a repressed homosexual (not denied) but also that he had a taste for exhibitionism and sadism and a narcissistic Christ-complex which disappeared only when the Turks captured and flogged him, forcing him to realize he was not superhuman.

A slightly different interpretation was advanced in Terence Rattigan's earlier play ''Ross''. It suggested that Lawrence was raped by a Turkish officer and that the shock of discovering a hidden weakness for sensuality drove him to abandon a brilliant career for the obscurity of post-war life as an enlisted man. Colonel Lawrence did in fact mysteriously shed his rank, first to join the Royal Tank Corps under the name of ''Ross'' and then the RAF under the name of ''Shaw'', working humbly there from 1925 until his death in a motor-cycle accident 10 years later. More conventional explanations of this are that he suffered a spiritual exhaustion after his desert exploits and the writing of his monumental book, ''The Seven Pillars of Wisdom'' – and that his exaggerated love of power expressed itself in an equally exaggerated renunciation of status after the war.

Whatever the truth, Lawrence was a man of fascinating complexity – an academic man of action, a sensual ascetic, a gregarious hermit and a vain hero who at the same time shunned public adulation. He was the son of an Irish baronet, born in North Wales and educated at Oxford. Pre-war archaeological studies familiarised him with the Middle East and led to his later being chosen to investigate the possibility of an Arab uprising. The portraits of Lawrence in his turban, his secret-agent string-pulling and military exploits, appealed irresistibly to the exotic fantasies of his own countrymen. And he embodied so many male qualities of courage, imagination and endurance that women will take a good deal of persuading that he cannot, in time, be turned into a sex symbol as well. The process of romanticism has already begun.

John Lindsay would be a front-runner for President if the decision were left to women voters. His finely-chiselled movie-star profile, his 6ft 3in elegance, his blue eyes, his famous twisted grin and his air of cool, affable, self-assurance constitute a package of male assets more potent than anything seen on the American political scene since John F. Kennedy, with whom he is often compared. His handsome family of five has the same kind of charisma.

If anything, Lindsay had a more independent and liberal voting record as a republican Congressman than Kennedy did as a Democrat. A Yale graduate in law and an ex-Navy lieutenant, he entered Congress in 1958. He offended the political establishment by repudiating Goldwaterism in 1964 but won a stunning victory for the New York mayoralty the following year as an Independent Republican. For a while, his dash, style and wit and the personal courage with which he faced racial and labour problems seemed to be just what the city needed. But the burdens of running a city required practical solutions he was unable to find. Critics said his administration had more image than substance. And he lost a lot of support when he rashly offered himself for the White House in 1972, only a year after switching to the Democratic Party. Whether he has lost his appeal as the white knight of American politics remains to be seen. By stepping down from the mayoralty at the end of last year, Lindsay left himself with his options open and most of his vote-winning capacity still intact.

John Lindsay, liberal America's new white hope until his bid for the Presidency in 1972 led to ''Anyone but Lindsay'' buttons. He's still the ladies' choice.

Norman Mailer, with his wild halo of greying curls, his stocky, overweight boxer's body, his boyish grin and his bossy, staccato voice, looks what he is – the rogue elephant of American letters. His exuberance, his hard-living hard-hitting reputation and his stream of dogmatic, arresting opinions about everything from politics to sex, make him the dominant figure at any party of literary celebrities and a man to whom women find it hard not to gravitate.

The extrovert part of him is New York Jewish. The intellectualism is rooted in New England. He was born in 1923, studied engineering at Harvard, served with the infantry in World War II and at 25 produced the toughest and best novel of that war, *The Naked and the Dead.* By 1967, he had written seven books and a play and was ready to prove his stamina by becoming a journalistic dynamo, striking off thousands of white-hot words on everything from the moon programme to Marilyn Monroe. In between, he offered himself as New York's first "existentialist" mayor. "Divorce is imperative if you want to know a woman", he says. He himself has had three divorces, four marriages. A *Nova* interviewer raved about his "sexy, male, deep-sea eyes". His critics accuse him of frantic self-advertisement and of using his teeming brain to cash in on American obsessions instead of subjecting himself to intellectual discipline. But to women, Mailer seems to represent mental energy in its most angry, virile form – a sort of literary equivalent of Mick Jagger.

Norman Mailer, colourful and extroverted journalist and author. He told one interviewer that most men get tied up with women too early. "You have to be what you're going to become and then fall in love", he said.

The brooding look of James Mason as seen in "Fanny by Gaslight" (1943). He played a sadistic husband who is attempting to drive his wife mad, and women loved it.

James Mason said "I like a woman to kiss my hand when I strike her", in "They Were Sisters" (1945). Though kinky sensuality is far more overt now than it was then, Mason is still the only film star to have based his romantic appeal on sadistic masculinity. His thundercloud brow, dark, brooding eyes and broad lips produced an extraordinary audience response from the moment he began laying about Margaret Lockwood with a riding crop in "The Man in Grey" (1943). His hate-and-hurt love affair with the same actress in "The Wicked Lady" and his cruelty to Jean Kent in "Fanny by Gaslight" only increased his following.

Mason himself seems to have both disliked this image and used it to further his career. After soaring to the top of the box office in Britain in 1947 he began being mean and moody off the screen as well as on it. He left for Hollywood, snarling at Rank and Korda for the way they ran the British film industry, and was then alternately rude and condescending about America. The iconoclastic image was popular with columnists who wrote endlessly about Mason, his profusion of clothes and cats, his talented wife, Pamela Kellino and his equally talented small daughter, Portland, who was said to hold her own in witty chat at late-night parties. But his hopes of becoming a leading man in Hollywood were disappointed. It was only in the 1950s that his gifts as a character actor of subtlety and strength began to be used.

James Neville Mason (born 1909) is the son of a wealthy Huddersfield wool merchant who sent him to Marlborough College where he was an outstanding student, a prefect and a flautist of some promise. After taking an architectural degree at Cambridge he became interested in the stage in 1931 and acted with the Old Vic and the Dublin Gate Theatre. He worked with his future wife on the script of a play and film in 1937. Since their divorce in 1964, Mason has lived mainly in Switzerland. He married an Australian actress, Clarissa Kaye, in 1971. In recent films he has deployed a weary charm which still echoes the sensuous quality that made him such an unusual heart-throb a quarter of a century earlier.

Marcello Mastroianni is a paradox in that he has spent most of his career making fun of the Latin lover of matinee fantasy and yet is persistently mistaken for the thing he is parodying. Fan magazines which call him "the greatest screen lover since Valentino" overlook the fact that in most of his films he plays men who are insecure, jaded, neurotic and more often victims of women than conquerors.

Mastroianni's enormous popularity, both inside Italy and internationally, rests on his ability to portray with tragi-comic finesse, many of the anxieties of an age in which sex roles are rapidly changing. His is the appeal of male weakness and indecisiveness rather than he-man strength and aggressiveness. The praise of one of his co-stars, Pamela Tiffin, is revealing: "He's romantic, he's sensual, he's elegant, he's a Latin lover and yet he's a Teddy bear too. There's something cuddly about him. And that voice! It makes your bones vibrate." It is Mastroianni's cuddly quality that is the essence of his attraction. His languorous, worried, brown eyes suggest to women that the frustration and impotence he suffers in his films could be solved by sympathetic treatment at their hands and that he would then be a patient, considerate and passionate lover.

He is the son of an Italian cabinet maker, born at Fontana, Liri, in 1923. After working as a draughtsman

Marcello Mastroianni, the antithesis of the callous, decisive lover as represented by James Bond, has become popular in an age of male anxiety. He has the exceptional talent of portraying a mood of tragi-comedy in most of his roles including the lead in "La Dolce Vita".

and commercial artist, he began a stage career after the war and moved into films in 1947. He was married in 1950. His bland face and weary charm made him the perfect choice as the central figure in Fellini's "La Dolce Vita" – a journalist drawn towards the effete pleasures of Roman society but finding no satisfaction in them. In "Yesterday, Today and Tomorrow" (1963), he is alternatively exploited and frustrated by Sophia Loren who calls him a "fairy" when he is unable to keep her in a state of perpetual pregnancy. In "Divorce Italian Style", he plays a narcisstic cuckold. In "Casanova 70" he is so kinky that he is able to make love only in situations of extreme peril – in a lion's cage or in the midst of a burglary.

Of his film roles he has said: "The characters are connected by cowardice. They don't do to life; life does to them." Mastroianni's real achievement is that he has given humorous expression to the sexual problems raised by women's liberation. For the first time in recent history, women have begun to make sexual advances to men. It is a reversal of accepted roles that might have disconcerted Casanova himself.

Victor Mature bared his magnificent torso in the film world of the 1940s. His deltoid muscles were always seen through a torn shirt or skimpy slave's tunic, straining against ropes, chains or fainting women. To some, his curly black hair, sensual mouth and curving nostrils were the embodiment of beefcake vulgarity and conceit. But publicity stills of ''the Hunk'' were pinned up by working girls throughout the early post-war years. Though critics found it hard to take him seriously after ''Samson and Delilah (1949), he was always rather good at tough, sinister roles and had enough humour to appear in a 1966 send-up of his own image, ''After the Fox''. Mature, who now concentrates mainly on his golf swing, was born in Louisville in 1916, went to California to study acting and won his first film role in 1939. He has been married four times.

Victor Mature in ''The Robe'' (1953), the first film in cinemascope. He was to bare his wide-screen chest in a sequel two years later, ''Demetrius and the Gladiators''.

Steve McQueen, enigma. During the shooting of his 1972 film, ''Le Mans'', one of the drivers working on the record of the 24-hour race said he had the feeling the whole thing had been set up so that McQueen could play with cars. His little-boy quality may be the essence of McQueen's allure for woman – the charm of a man who continually has to pretend he is tougher and more independent than he really feels. He plays at being a danger man more seriously than most would care to. His creased, lived-in face, the scars on his head, nose and lip, his wary blue eyes, all testify to the bumps he had taken on the way to becoming one of the two or three most potent sex symbols on the contemporary screen. He expresses his obsession with danger for its own sake with romantic fervour: ''Speed is incredible and beautiful. Slip-streaming around a turn in the middle of the pack is what separates the men from the boys. If you can't cut in you have to back out. It's as simple as that. And that's life.''

The first man to back out of Terence Steven McQueen's life was his father who deserted his wife and six-month old son in Indiannapolis in 1930. The boy went to his grand-parents on a Missouri farm. When he later rejoined his mother in California he found he could not get on with his stepfather. Juvenile hell-raising eventually landed him in a reform school at Chino. After two years there he moved on to work as a deck boy, lumberjack and brothel-runner (in Port Arthur at the age of 15). He began his love affair with machinery in the Marine Corps from 1947 to 1950. An ex-serviceman's scholarship took him to drama school after he had become interested in the stage while working as a television repair man in Greenwich Village. He showed enough talent to be accepted for the Actor's Studio three years later and to win a Broadway role in ''A Hatful of Rain'' in 1956. His film career began after an attractively off-beat characterization as Josh Reynolds, the bounty hunter of the television series ''Wanted – Dead or Alive'', which he began playing in 1958.

It was ''The Great Escape'' (1963) which established McQueen's screen personality as a quiet, casually-daring loner. He played an American POW who goes his own way rather than join an over-organised breakout planned by British officers and gets as far as the Swiss border on a motor-cycle ridden with breath-taking skill. McQueen was good enough on a motor-cycle to represent America in the 1964 six-day cross-country championships in Germany. He has also raced sports cars for John Cooper and BMC. His Porsche took second place in its class at Sebring in 1970.

The identification with speed is one part of McQueen's sex appeal. The chase sequences in ''Bullitt'' (1968) when he slammed a sports car sickeningly down the roller-coaster avenues of San Francisco produced an immediate surge of box-office popularity. His other attraction is the tension he sets up by combining an impression of restless velocity with a surface appearance of calmness. However reckless the characters he plays, they are never brash, cocky or overtly violent. His lined cheeks, mild blue eyes and neat faun's head, his dry, pursed lips and sudden grin, are disarming rather than tough. He is compact and wiry, moves lightly, ready to jump. Like Paul Newman, he has that indefinable personal style which is hip, cool, aware.

"I don't dig love scenes. They're not for real", he told an interviewer. Yet the electricity was crackling when he and Faye Dunaway played cat and mouse in "The Thomas Crown Affair" and in "The Getaway", when his co-star was his present wife, Ali McGraw. (His earlier marriage to the Broadway dancer and singer, Neile Adams, mother of his two children, broke up in 1971 after 15 years). McQueen believes he attracts young people because he has spent a lifetime fighting the Establishment. With a salary of about $1 million a film, and with his own company, Solar Productions, since 1965, he is on the way to becoming something of an establishment himself. But he guards his independence fiercely, takes physical risks when his insurance company will let him, and keeps aloof socially. In his mid-40s, he manages still to retain the aura of rebelliousness he brought with him from reform school.

Below *Steve McQueen in "The Great Escape",*
following his daring ride over fields and hills on a
motor-cycle in an attempt to get away from the Germans.

Right *McQueen's competitive spirit and driving skill*
could have made him a world-class racing driver, say
professionals who worked with him in the film "Le Mans".

Robert Mitchum, one of the generation of film stars who emerged in the 1940s, is among the few whose personal style was still gaining admirers instead of losing them 20 years later. He has the charm of contradiction and enigma. His cleft-chinned face with its heavy-lidded eyes and flick of hair and his well-developed physique suggest aggression, yet his screen presence is quiet, even kind. His manner is laconic, flip and cynical, yet he writes poems and ballads and seems to care. In 1948, Mitchum served 59 days of a sentence of marijuana possession. Though the sentence was reviewed and the charge expunged in 1951, the image of a social rebel has stuck and become an asset. His self-mockery also chimes with contemporary fashions in heroism. He says people think "If that great slob can be a movie star, I can be king. I represent hope." And he told one interviewer that he only went into films because he thought he could do better than Rin-Tin-Tin.

A restless childhood left Mitchum with a cool, tough exterior and the habit of loneliness. (His wife Dorothy, whom he married in 1940, called him "the most married bachelor in Hollywood" because he was always going off fishing or camping). He was born in Bridgeport, Connecticut, in 1917, was unhappy with a stepfather and left school at 14 to become a hobo, working variously as a labourer and once on a Georgia road gang. Before entering films in 1943, he was working in an aircraft factory and as a ghost-writer. His solidity as a leading man was first recognized in "The Story of G.I. Joe" (1945). Charles Laughton paid tribute to his expressive underplaying after producing him in "The Night of the Hunter" (1955) and his quiet power made him a dominant figure in Westerns of the 1960s.

Robert Mitchum in "The Big Steal". Nine years as a hobo and 30 as a film star, he calls himself a male version of the "whore with the heart of gold" fantasy. Those who know him say the gentleness is genuine.

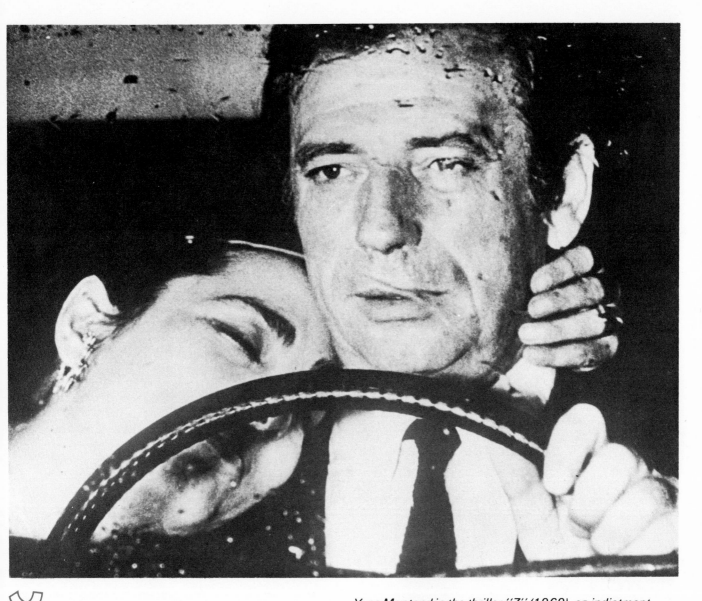

ves Montand beat the system. In the late 1950s, Hollywood tried hard to turn him into a light romantic actor – a cross between Maurice Chevalier and Charles Boyer. He was France's best cafe singer and actor and Marilyn Monroe was calling him "the most exciting man I've ever met". But Montand could not be forced into a conventional celluloid mould. Nor could Marilyn (he called her "an enchanting child") break up his long, volatile marriage to Simone Signoret. He went back to France in 1964 to resume an acting career that would produce a definitive performance in "Z" (1969) as a world-weary leftwing political leader.

Montand is the most attractively-ugly screen hero since Humphrey Bogart. His tough, seamed face with its paunched, sleepy eyes and crooked teeth can look like a tired labourer's. But he can also be suave, sophisticated and humorous. "His casual virility curls the toes of every woman in the audience", said a critic of his one-man show on Broadway. Majorie Proops went to lunch with

Yves Montand in the thriller "Z" (1969), an indictment of totalitarian government which was interpreted as a criticism of the military junta in Greece.

him and said he "makes you feel his day is made because he's eating lamb chops with *you*".

Montand is actually from Italy. He was born Ivo Livi in 1921 and was taken to Marseilles by his peasant-Jewish family after the rise of Mussolini. He left school at 11, then got to know the back streets of Marseilles as a barman, barber's assistant, docker and vaudeville artist. His singing brought him in touch with Edith Piaf who fell in love with him and made him her protegé in 1945. He appeared in "Les Portes de la Nuit" in 1946, built up a reputation as a ballad singer and became an international star in "The Wages of Fear" (1955) with an unforgettable portrayal of a washed-up cynic who recovers his willpower in a last, doomed enterprise. Montand is an outspoken Marxist, but was appalled at the Russian invasion of Czechoslovakia and in 1970 announced that he was not a member of the Communist Party.

Audie Murphy was the epitome of valour in modern warfare which more often leads to death than fame. America has good reason to cherish the boy, who, in World War II, won 24 decorations before his 21st birthday. He returned looking absurdly small, young and cheerful and was idolised with all the hunger of a nation eager to believe that the old myth was still true; that a small-town boy could sail away, perform great deeds and come home safe.

Audie had been one of nine Texas backwoods children whose father had deserted them and whose mother died when he was 16. The Marines and paratroops told him he was undersized and under-age when he tried to enlist, but at 18 he became a private in the 7th Army. Once in action, he began to display astonishing initiative and dash, once capturing a hill and machine-gun post alone and in a still more spectacular exploit, leaping on to a burning tank destroyer and holding off six German tanks and advancing infantry. Among other decorations, he won the Medal of Honour and the DSC. He was wounded three times and in 30 months of combat rose to 2nd lieutenant and was said to have killed or captured 250 Germans.

His open, freckled face with its shock of red hair appeared to bear no trace of what he had done and seen. In 1955, when he played the hero of his own story in the film "To Hell and Back" he looked unconvincingly young for the role. The war had nevertheless left its mark. His film career, which began in 1945, declined steadily after the mid-1950s into low-budget Westerns. And though he made a successful marriage with his second wife Pamela Archer (his first was film star Wanda Hendrix), he found it hard to adjust to life without a cause. He attached himself to the Los Angeles police as a self-appointed special agent crusading against drugs. In 1970, he survived a charge of attempted murder for beating up a man he thought had mistreated a dog. He died when his private plane crashed the following year. On the whole, the public is happier with fictional than with real-life heroes. Audie Murphy himself, seemed uncomfortable in the role of America's No. 1 war hero. Not long before his death, he confessed that he had felt tired ever since the war ended.

Ilie Nastase's claim to be the best tennis player in the world was consolidated only recently. But well before that he had become the most magnetic champion since Pancho Gonzales. To a sport which was being increasingly dominated by methodical power players he restored adventure, cunning, imagination, high spirits and even villainy.

The following of girls he collects at his tournaments is partly a tribute to his physical attraction – the lithe, rubbery build, the classical jaw, the dimples, the olive green eyes under the long, dark hair. But it is his complex, emotional personality that supplies most of his sexuality, a nervous tension which expresses itself either in pantherish concentration or in temperamental play-acting. He shuffles around pigeon-toed, he hides his eyes, he glares, he mocks linesmen, he waves his arms, he talks to his wife, Dominique, who sits nearby, looking like a young Bardot, shouting warnings or encouragement. She is French. To the despair of his fans,

Audie Murphy as he was when he came home from the war at the age of 20, laden with military honours, to be lionised by patriotic societies throughout America. His freckles and red hair had an unusual appeal.

he married her in 1972 after years as an elusive amorist.

Nastase is a Bucharest bank officer's son, was born there in 1946, started playing tennis at 11 and began his international career in 1966, partnering another formidable Rumanian player, Ion Tiriac. Like Muhammed

Ilie Nastase, the Rumanian extrovert whose temperament has become part of his tactics on the tennis court. Nicknamed "Nasty" by opponents – but not by the girls, his appeal derives from his native energy and spirit.

Ali, he infuriates people who expect sportsmen to behave correctly. And like Ali, his displays of temper and his child-like delight when he is playing well, are also the essence of his appeal. His uncanny anticipation and his loose-wristed, sleight-of-hand shots seem less the product of a well-disciplined body and mind than of pure freakish talent. In an age of over-trained, over-regulated sportsmen, Nastase is a heart-throb because he appears to represent the triumph of a more instinctive, more primitive energy and spirit.

Paul Newman is in his late 40s now, but the blue eyes still jolt, the youthful profile with its short, jutting nose, neat mouth and hard jaw still looks carved from Greek marble. After nearly 20 years in films, Newman's has become the unchanging face on the shoulders of a long line of fictional sex-heroes, each characterization heightening his superstar charisma. When polls tell him he is the man most women would like for a lover he grins wryly and says he is happily married.

Robert Shaw, who co-starred with him in his 1973 film, ''The Sting'', thinks Newman has the same kind of theatrical presence as Laurence Olivier, an indefinable magnetism. It is the product of a strong individuality asserting itself in every role he plays. The odd thing is that Newman was written off in the mid-1950s as just another Marlon Brando – possibly because he seemed to have many of Brando's mannerisms in the 1956 film which first brought him to notice, ''The Rack''. It was only in 1958 when he made Ben Quick such a lean, smart, dangerous character in ''The Long Hot Summer'', that Newman emerged as a formidable new screen personality. In the next few years he quarrelled with his studio (Warners), went back to Broadway to rock audiences in ''Sweet Bird of Youth'' and then starred in ''The Hustler'', the 1961 film which finally established the Newman-style hero – shrewd, sexually-assured, truculent and coldly charming.

Newman's father was a successful sports goods store owner in Cleveland where Paul was born in 1925. After service in the navy flying torpedo planes, he graduated BA in 1949, married Jackie Witte, did some stock acting and liked it so much that he gave up the sports goods store in 1951 to study first at the Yale School of Drama and then at Actors' Studio. He was understudying in ''Picnic'' when he met Joanne Woodward, for whom he was to give up his first wife and three children to remarry in 1958. He was the product of a Catholic-Jewish background and felt very guilty. He and Joanne also have three children. They live and work together in a harmony which seems to be based on the balance of two strong egos. Apart from their acting together, Newman has directed his wife in two films with outstanding results. ''Rachel, Rachel'' (1968) won him the New York Critics' Award as best director. He formed a production company, First Artists, with other stars in 1969.

It is as a symbol of cool, tough, self-reliant masculinity that Newman has won his huge following. By the 1950s, audiences had become used to the concept of the heel-hero. Clark Gable had told Vivien Leigh ''Frankly my

Paul Newman in ''Pocket Money'' (1972). His clear blue eyes, mellifluous voice and athletic body have attracted women of all ages for many years. His appeal is still apparent in his recent film, ''The Sting''.

dear, I don't give a damn'', at the end of ''Gone With the Wind'' as early as 1939. To Newman, however, fell the dubious honour of creating a character who was, according to his own lights, both successful and attractive without having a single redeeming virtue. As Hud in the 1962 film of the same name, he was the cold-blooded, dishonest, disloyal, amoral and egocentric son of a respected cattle baron. Posters for the film called him the man with the ''barbed-wire soul''. What was unusual about the film was the casting of Newman, a recognized screen hero, in a villain role and the cynical realism of showing him as the film's ultimate survivor. Though Hud was a man without conscience, warmth or compassion, hungry only for sex and power, Newman's physical chemistry made him seem more attractive than repellent. And the fact that the film increased Newman's own popularity suggests that ''Hud'' accurately gauged a mood of its time.

He returned to a more conventional hero role in ''Cool-Hand Luke'' (1967) as a harmless delinquent who gets on the wrong side of the law at its most brutal. When the prison system tries to break his spirit, Luke submits to punishment with an infuriating smile. Like Marlon Brando, Newman seems to have a fascination for roles in which he is beaten up. Both of them are appealing to a long tradition of the hero as a sacrificial victim. Newman has lately said he feels he may be getting stale. But he has the capacity to outlive the hard-muscled, all-American looks, the dazzling smile and the arrogance that gave him such a glamorous image in the 1960s. In comedy roles, his charm once seemed rather too knowing. Films like ''Butch Cassidy and the Sundance Kid'' and ''The Sting'' have shown him mellowing into a man who can underplay with hip ease.

David Niven's instant reaction when asked to say something for a screen test in 1935 was to recite in his impeccable, clipped, English accent a dirty limerick about an old man from Leeds. He has made a career out of being stylishly outrageous ever since. His quizzical eyebrows, dapper moustache and urbane, unflappable charm make him the sort of older man who causes tremors in office typing pools and among daughters asked to dinner by their father's business friends.

It was ironic that Niven should win an Oscar playing a furtive pervert in ''Separate Tables'' (1958). On the evidence of his exhilarating autobiography, ''The Moon's A Balloon'', his own sex-life has been one long romp since the age of 14. He was born in Kirriemuir, Scotland, in 1909 and as a boy tried the patience of several school headmasters as well as a stuffy stepfather who tried to supervise him after his own father was killed in the Gallipoli campaign. After Sandhurst training as an officer and a dreary stretch of army life on Malta, he lived on his wits for several years in America before gravitating to

Hollywood where one of his earliest off-screen exploits was to get his polo stick wedged under the tail of Darryl Zanuck's horse during a game which Niven turned into a shambles.

Between drunken or amorous escapades off-screen, he established himself as a light comedian of effortless, if heartless polish as well as a specialist in tight-lipped British heroics. He rejoined the British army at the outbreak of war and met his first wife, Primmie. She died tragically in a fall at a party soon after their return to Hollywood. He married his present wife, Hjordes, in 1948 and they have lived with their family at Cap Ferrat for some years. Niven, the debonair, middle-aged playboy, was seen at his most formidable in "The Moon Is Blue" (1953). Unlike some of his contemporaries who have preserved a Dorian Gray smoothness, Niven's face reflects in its whorls and wrinkles, the scalliwag charm of a man who looks as if he sees life as a sex comedy and has played his own role in it with considerable joie-de-vivre.

Rudolph Nureyev entranced London, when he first danced at Drury Lane; crowds waiting to see him blocked traffic. In New York, giggling girls chanted "We want Rudi, especially in the nudi." Only in Russia, where his defection to the West has never really been forgiven, is Rudolph Nureyev not acknowledged as the most glamorous male ballet dancer in memory and the best since Nijinsky.

Nureyev's dramatic break with the Leningrad Kirov Ballet in 1960 described by the newspapers as a "leap to freedom". But it involved few political motives. The company, then dancing in Paris, felt Nureyev's head had been turned and that he was becoming an undisciplined star, impatient with ensemble work and sulky if he was given subordinate roles. He was recalled to Leningrad. At the air terminal, he suddenly broke away and ran leaping and shouting through the terminal demanding asylum. When he began dancing in London, he was surrounded with the phosphorescent halo of a rebel hero. Nureyev's faun-like face with its high cheekbones, vivid dark eyes and sensual pouting mouth reflects his Tartar extraction. He was born in the Ural mountains in 1937, began dancing as a child in Uffa and in his teens went to Moscow with a folk-dance company. After only three years study with the Leningrad ballet, he was a star, producing soaring, suspended leaps that were later to astonish London audiences.

His dancing combines passionate and elemental

Above *David Niven in his role as Raffles in a film after the same name directed by Sam Goldwyn. In his autobiography, he claimed to have once introduced his girlfriend (a London street-walker) to his public school headmaster, who was completely charmed.*

As an actor, he has establed himself as a light comedian of effortless polish and as a specialist in tight-lipped British heroics.

Right *The great Rudolph Nureyev dancing in "The Corsair". One critic, searching for words to describe his masculine-feminine quality, called Nureyev "part Garbo, part Genghis Khan". His classic grace and balance are apparent when he performs on the stage.*

virility with a sensitive doe-like quality. Apart from his unusual balance of masculine strength and feminine grace, it was the emotional abandon of his dancing that most struck critics used to the colder style of Western ballet. A "Rimbaud of the Steppes", said Frederick Ashton. One critic, searching for words to describe the attractive masculine-feminine quality of Nureyev, called him "part Garbo, part Genghis Khan". It was this combination of strength, which reflected the broad sweep of his Russian heritage, and sensitivity which was communicated through dance, that created his immense attraction.

Off-stage, he behaved like Royalty. He was capricious, narcissistic, sullen, mischievous. His years with the Royal Ballet and his long, marvellous partnership with Margot Fonteyn have matured him without removing his boyishness. He has become cool, soft-spoken and sometimes almost sombre, but on stage retains most of the spring and velocity,

Laurence Olivier's mystery is why a man who for 40 years has been able to turn women's knees to jelly both on and off the stage did not become a dominating screen hero at the beginning of the 1940s when he played several saturnine roles in Hollywood, beginning with "Wuthering Heights" and "Rebecca". Was his image too intellectual, too steel-edged and too frightening to become the stuff of mass romantic fantasy? Or was he simply out-of-step with heart-throbs of the forties?

What the screen lost, the stage gained – a man of such dynamic theatrical presence that critics were using the word "great" about him long before his career had reached its peak in the 1960s. Someone even used it

Laurence Olivier, Titan of the British theatre (seen here with Greer Garson in "Pride and Prejudice"), once seemed likely to dominate Hollywood as well.

about him when he was only 10 – Ellen Terry. She saw him playing Brutus in a church production and told his father, a stern minister himself given to preaching dramatic sermons, that the boy should go on the stage. He was born in 1907, and his mother died when he was 12. After school in London and Oxford, he trained at the Central School of Speech and Drama, began acting in the West end and appeared in his first film in 1930. He was then moodily handsome in a dark, sullen Italianate way and Hollywood decided to match him with Greta Garbo in "Queen Christina" (1933). To his horror, she froze during their first love scene. Olivier was replaced.

Back in Britain, he had fluctuating success on the stage and in films. He married Vivien Leigh in 1940, served in the Fleet Air Arm and during the war also began

The young Olivier; he's had his ups and downs despite his formidable acting gifts. A New York critic once called his portrayal of Romeo "the worst ever".

his revival of Shakespeare as a living force in the cinema. His productions of "Henry V", "Richard III" and "Hamlet", his reconstruction of the Old Vic company after the war, his directorship of the National Theatre (1962-1973) and his succession of outstanding performances during these years revealed a man of unusual energy and imagination as well as an actor of remarkable range and tragi-comic skill. In 1961 he married Joan Plowright, now mother of his three children. In 1970, he became the first life peer of the theatre.

Olivier has always radiated vitality. He likes verbal surprises and physical stunts – once astonishing audiences with a full somersault during the death scene in "Coriolanus". The daemonic energy, the cutting precision of his voice, the air of male authority are leavened now with an instinctive feeling for human weakness which may have been the only missing element in the Olivier with whom Hollywood could never quite come to terms.

ristotle Onassis? "Look, he's just a little guy", some irritated American is supposed to have said to his wife after Onassis married Jackie Kennedy. "Not when he stands on his money", she answered. Without it, Onassis is 5ft 3in. In his late 60s, his heavy-lidded, almond-shaped eyes are sunk in deep pouches behind his thick spectacles. His black hair is greying and his stocky wrestler's body is shaped like a box. But anybody who does not find Onassis a heart-throb has to explain how he has managed to love three of the most formidable beauties of his time and marry two of them. Maria Callas, who was the woman in his life after his 1960 divorce from Tina Livanos and until his 1968 marriage to Jackie, said he was "full of life and glamour". Friends speak of his combination of toughness and fairness, his friendliness, his wit and his masterful style. He swears like a stevedore, thinks like a poet and knows about books and art as well as business and politics.

Onassis told an interviewer the three simple rules for success in life were to walk upright, maintain a deep suntan and smile a lot. Few other tanned, upright, grinning men have managed to turn $60 into nearly a billion dollars. The male qualities that really seem to distinguish Onassis are energy, adventurousness and imagination. He was born in 1906 of Greek parents in Smyrna where his father was a wealthy tobacco merchant. But when the Turks retook the city in 1922 (hanging three of his uncles), the family had to restart. At 16, Onassis was sent off to Buenos Aires with a few dollars which he increased within two years to $100,000 by working as a phone operator at night and organizing a tobacco importing business by day. At 25, he had branched out into wool, hides, grain and oil and was a millionaire. During the Depression, he bought six cheap oil tankers nobody else wanted and seeing war coming began rapidly adding to a tanker fleet that would dominate Allied sea routes along with the tankers of two other Greeks, Stavros Livanos and Stavros Niarchos.

He married Tina Livanos (then 17) in 1946 and entered a tanker-building race against Niarchos. By 1955, he owned 90 vessels and headed 30 companies. In one notable demonstration of his determination, he bought the Monte Carlo casino when it would not sell him a clubhouse he wanted near his chateau in the Antibes.

Onassis, who is said to love rare, beautiful and unattainable things, was 63 when he married Jackie Kennedy. Fascinated gossip columnists investigated his 65-crew yacht, his seaplane, his palace on the private island of Scorpios and his wife's shopping bills and claimed the honeymoon year had cost him about £8 million.

His enemies say that Aristotle Onassis has a "Goliath complex". Women friends say "He grows on you and begins to seem almost handsome".

Donny Osmond, for the 8-15 age-bracket, is the one member of the six Osmond brothers who is "just right" – halfway between the dwarfish cuteness of sub-teen Jimmy and the more masculine image of the older boys. Overt masculinity is not what the teeny-boppers want. Like David Cassidy, Donny Osmond is their heart-throb because his sexuality is not frightening. His big, brown eyes, lustrous hair, soft cheeks and unwavering smile make him as clean and cuddly as the Donny Osmond Sweet Dreams Pillowcases his fans can buy.

The Osmond parents deny that sexuality is part of the group's appeal at all. As dedicated Mormons, their mission is to be "friendly to the world". But nobody who has watched the Osmonds wiggling in their tight, white suits and grinding on the necks of their guitars can doubt that it is the rhythmic excitement of their performance that reduces their young audiences to dazed sobbing. The Osmonds themselves are a genuinely happy group who come from Salt Lake City and who were discovered in 1968 when the older boys were singing at Disneyland. In addition to being the most talented and appealing singer in the group, Donny, who was born in 1958, is gadget-mad and says he would be happy studying electronics if his star wanes (which seems unlikely at the moment).

Donny Osmond has been known to sustain his paralysing smile without a quiver while teeny-bopper fans tore the microphone from his hands.

Peter Seamus O'Toole shows how height and gentleness have a perennial attraction for women, and with the corn-coloured hair, the round, Irish-blue eyes, the wide mouth and long, square jaw, he has always looked unnervingly handsome as well – the sort of man a woman scientist might create to start a new breed of genetically perfect but not too brawny men.

A lapsed altar boy with guilty childhood memories of disapproving nuns, O'Toole is the son of a bookmaker in Connemara, Eire, where he was born in 1932. He left his North of England school at 14, did a spell in the navy, which he hated, and in the photographic department of a newspaper, which he liked, and then went to study at drama school after some repertory experience in Leeds. He joined the Bristol Old Vic in 1956, married actress Sian·Phillips in 1958 and by 1960 was the star of that year's Shakespearian season at Stratford. The visual splendour of "Lawrence of Arabia" (1963) turned him overnight into a kind of screen fairy prince.

The same film, he says, changed him from a rather noisy bohemian who had a compulsion to smash up cars into a more mature personality. Films like "Becket" (1964) and "The Lion in Winter" (1968) showed a lean strength and an acting range that had not been apparent in the winsome heroics of "Lawrence". O'Toole, who is now co-director of a film company, likes to escape when he can to Connemara with his wife and two children and says that since he is more interested in ideas than looks he is not a great ladies' man. He is, however, the spindly-limbed, doe-eyed, charming man of many ladies' dreams.

Gregory Peck's image on the screen is usually wreathed in the dependable aura of pipesmoke and tweed. His shoulders look made for children to climb on and women to cry on. During the 1940s and 1950s, his deep voice, his tall frame and his dark, earnest face embodied the kind of masculine solidity and gentle strength most women dreamed of finding in a post-war husband – if not a lover. The image won him an Oscar (after four earlier nominations) in "To Kill a Mockingbird" (1963).

He was born in La Jolla, California in 1916, drove a truck while studying at Berkeley and had some stage experience before moving into films in 1943. He has three children by his first marriage to Greta Konen and two by his French second wife, Veronique Passani, whom he met when she interviewed him for a Paris magazine. He has struck some other interviewers as rather humourless and pompous. But it was his patent honesty which always came through in his screen roles and made him a consistently likeable hero.

As a brute, he was not so convincing. David O.Selznick made the mistake of casting him as a reckless tearaway in "Duel in the Sun" (1946). His real forte was the slow-thinking good man, grappling with the problems of right and wrong in a complex world, a grave smile twitching the corners of his mouth. It was perfectly realized in "The Man in the Grey Flannel Suit", Sloan Wilson's story of a junior executive who is suddenly offered wealth and power but rejects them in favour of peace of mind. His playing of Ahab in "Moby Dick" the same year (1956) showed that he could also muster a good deal of brooding power without losing the qualities of quietness, economy and understatement which always distinguished his acting and his screen presence.

Above *Peter O'Toole as "Lawrence of Arabia", David Lean's six Oscar film. O'Toole said his experience of the desert and the Bedouin people changed the course of his life.*

Right *Gregory Peck won an Oscar for his performance in "To Kill a Mockingbird" (1963). The film dramatised Peck's defence of a black unjustly accused of murder in a prejudiced Southern community.*

erard Phillipe's death at 36 seemed all the more poignant because he was the golden boy of a postwar era in which only the Fench and Italians seemed to be producing worthwhile films. Unlike James Dean, he is remembered not because he expressed the contemporary nervous tics of his own generation but because he seemed to represent what is perpetual in youth – its gaiety, grace and tragic brevity. Many of his films were period pieces which allowed him to display the elegance and finesse of a training in classical theatre.

His amused green eyes, his fine features and dimples, might have condemned him to matinee-idol roles in Hollywood, but France was producing stylish films like ''La Ronde'' (1950) and ''Summer Manoeuvres'' (1955). Phillipe was able to progress from the soulful schoolboy he played in ''Le Diable au Corps'' (1946) to display a deep and adventurous talent. He was born in Cannes in 1922, thought of becoming a lawyer, but instead went to the Conservatory of Dramatic Art. He made his debut on the stage at 20 and often returned to it to act and later to direct. English newspapers called him ''Monsieur Heart-throb'' and reported after his death from cancer that hysterical fans had stolen his tombstone. But Gerard Phillipe appealed more to the romantic intellectual than to the mass market. His wife, Anne, has written a moving account of their life together.

A product of France, Gerard Phillipe emerged as a heart-throb through the cinema. His death from cancer at the age of 36 distressed his many fans.

Sidney Poitier has a bomb ticking away somewhere inside him which makes him one of the most explosive actors on the screen. The tension between his surface cool and his inner anger is perfectly expressed in all his physical movements – the velvet brown eyes which glow softly and then blaze, the long, boneless limbs which suddenly become rigid. It is this latent rage which distinguishes him as much as the colour of his skin, though he can never escape the implications of being a Negro – the first ever to become top at the box office (in 1968). A critic once called Poitier ''heroically inoffensive''. His poise and intelligence, his fine-featured 6ft 2in boyish looks and the succession of virtuous roles he played throughout the 1950s and 1960s identified him as a handsome figurehead for the civil rights movement rather than a disturbing racial threat. To white liberals, he was a comforting bridge between the comic Uncle Toms of Hollywood tradition and the big-lipped, broad-nosed Afro-cut reality of black militancy. In most of his films, he was shown as less violent, less aggressive and more moral than the white bigots against whom he was usually pitted. To make the liberal point, Negroes had to be portrayed almost as saints.

Poitier resents this over-simplification of the racial issue and has recently moved closer to the black separatists. But he has recognized also the need for gradualism. He wants to see more Negro actors established at the top before tackling deeper confrontations with Anglo-Saxon prejudices. He learnt caution through hard experience after he left his father's tomato farm in the West Indies at the age of 13 (in 1939) and crossed from Nassau to Miami. His refusal to be humble, which provoked a group of local police to beat him up – he had thumbed a lift in their patrol car. He worked as a delivery boy and a parking lot attendant, did other odd jobs in New York, was too rebellious to settle for a career as an army physiotherapist and finally found his way to the American Negro Theatre in 1944 (auditioning with an extract from a *True Confession* magazine he had been using to teach himself to read.)

He toured in ''Anna Lucasta'' (1947-49), then found himself everybody's favourite Negro after his first film, ''No Way Out'' in 1950. ''Lilies of the Field'' (1963) won him an Oscar. He has been married to Juanita Hardy since 1951 and is very like the character he portrays on the screen – likeable, dignified, intelligent and modestly unbothered about his magnetism for women.

Sidney Poitier in the 1963 film that won him an Oscar, "Lilies of the Field". It was the first Best Actor award to go to a Negro leading man. He was turned down when he first applied to join the Negro Theatre in 1943. He bought a radio and for six months trained himself to eliminate his West Indian accent. For script-reading practice, he used True Confession magazine.

Tyrone Power (1914-1958) was arguably the best-looking man ever to become a film actor of any authority. His graceful 6ft build, his dark hair and glowing brown eyes, his astonishingly regular features and his shattering smile were the sort of too-obvious looks that usually disqualify a man from anything more subtle than modelling work of B-grade costume romances. As it was, he had to struggle to avoid this fate and it was only after "The Razor's Edge" (1946) that he began to be taken seriously as an actor.

He was always, however, a heart-throb, projecting along with his portrayals of dashing courage, a baby face and a devastatingly gentle personality. He was born in Cincinnati into an Irish family with a long stage tradition and was on the stage himself at 17. Hollywood turned him down in 1932 but was happy to give him light romantic roles after 1936. He seemed to lack the passion for weightier roles. An attractive wryness began to emerge, however, when he returned to films in 1946 after service with the Marines. His 1949 marriage to Linda Christian and their audience with the Pope was ballyhooed almost as enthusiastically as their later divorce. Power was obsessed with carrying on the family stage tradition, but was denied either a great success on the stage himself or a son. Soon after he married for the third time (to Deborah Minardes) in 1958, he suffered a fatal heart attack. His French first wife, Ann Carpentier, called him "the most wonderful man in the world". He was certainly one of the most handsome.

Tyrone Power, whose dark, regular features made him the most popular pin-up of the 1940s. He never liked being type-cast in costume romances.

Elvis Aaron Presley stunned straight-laced American parents when he began swinging his hips, thumping his guitar and hollering "Bee-bop-belulah" in the mid-1950s. He lifted the animal sexuality of Negro blues out of the basement clubs and unleashed it across the world on millions of spinning pick-up turntables a full eight years before the pop-rock tide of the Beatles and the Rolling Stones began rolling.

By all the conventions of his day, Elvis "the Pelvis" was a shuddering compendium of male vulgarity – the sort of street-corner and pool-saloon yokel daughters might bring home in their parents' nightmares. His heavy-lidded, spoiled-Greek profile, his flicking cowlick of greasy black hair with its long sideburns, the clashing colours he wore, the insolent, threatening sensuality of his music was the antithesis of the civilized, dinner-jacketed crooners who had dominated popular music since the beginning of the jazz era. And therein lay Presley's enormous attraction for his own generation. He was an outlaw. Instead of adult wit, poise, charm, control, he preached the supremacy of the adolescent forces – uninhibited power, energy, noise, rebellion, anarchy, sex.

His parents were poor, God-fearing share-croppers from the Deep South town of Tulepo, Mississippi, where Elvis was born (with a stillborn twin brother) in January, 1935. The family moved to Memphis when he was 13 and it was there that he began hanging around local clubs, listening to Blues and country music, trying out with his own guitar at night after work as a truck-driver. He had cut five singles when he met a small-time promoter named Colonel Tom Parker who negotiated a contract with RCA-Victor and began the shrewd publicity campaign that would produce within the next three years all the symptoms of Presleymania – the flood of hit records (seven on the charts in one week alone), the "I Love Elvis" buttons, the films and the carefully-rationed personal appearances with their ambulances, security guards and hysterical audiences.

Beneath the public image of arrogance and aggression, Presley himself was a polite, well-behaved, manageable, even patriotic, country boy. After his two years in the army (1958-60), his promoters began a gradual shift away from hard rock towards the middle-of-the-road film and nightclub market in which he is now firmly and profitably established. His move to respectability was confirmed when he got married (though it ended in divorce). His mellow voice and his musical taste have outlived the era of the tight pants and garish jackets, the yellow and pink Cadillacs and the ominous violence of "Jailhouse Rock". But it was the sullen, tigerish Presley of that era who was the heart-throb, not the sleek, well-heeled glamour boy of Las Vegas.

The most significant difference between Presley and the later rock heroes is that he was a fantasy lover – the

Elvis Presley, the golden boy of the pop charts in the mid-50s. His panting voice established a thrilling secret between the singer and listener and his impact on the teen-age heart has seldom been equalled.

musical equivalent of Valentino. Behind his entourage of male friends and the high walls of his house, he was inaccessible. He appeared seldom and revealed very little about his private life or views. And though his movements on stage were blunt, his music was more suggestive than blatantly sexual. The words were often moony and innocuous. They became sensual because Presley's panting voice established a thrilling secret between singer and listener. His broken ''luh-huvs'' and ''hu-holds'' and his mid-song murmurs of gratification were a kind of pillow-talk which made him a surrogate boyfriend, closer and more passionate than the real one was usually allowed to be.

nthony Quinn as Zorba the Greek. "To dance, one must be a little mad." Anthony Rudolph Oaxaca Quinn, who played Zorba in the 1964 film, is not only a superb natural dancer. His personal outlook is so close to Zorba's that he inevitably became a guru of the flower generation – the only screen actor of his age to identify himself so whole-heartedly with the hippy philosophy of living first and worrying about the consequences later. Quinn's appeal was a change from the film hero of the 1950s who, more often than not, emerged as a figure from the Establishment.

His Mexican-Irish family came to Los Angeles from Chihuahua, Mexico, where Quinn was born in 1915. His father, a cameraman, got him a part as a juvenile Tarzan in a jungle film. At 14 he was already hefty enough to take on Depression-time jobs ranging from boxing to ditch digging. An operation to cure a speech impediment then opened the way for a film career which began when he was 20 with a succession of roles as ignoble savages, exploiting the strength of his 6ft 3in physique and his dark, ferocious face. A 1938 marriage to Katherine, the adopted daughter of Cecil B. De Mille produced four children but did not survive his emergence in the late 1950s as a kind of gusty, unshaven, arm-waving Earth Father, sowing wild oats on and off the screen. He married the Italian mother of his second son in the 1960s.

Quinn became an international star in 1954 with a shattering performance as the dumb-ox sideshow strongman in "La Strada" who experiences love and loss only with the uncomprehending pain of an animal. Two years later he played Gauguin in "Lust for Life" and became the screen embodiment of the free spirit. "Zorba the Greek" consolidated his image as the ageless romantic, drinking, laughing, loving, philosophising, crushing women in bearish hugs, smashing furniture or noses as the impulse takes him. Hun or hunchback, saint or sinner, Italian peasant or Mexican bandit, Quinn represents the elemental life-force in every role he plays. Not surprisingly, his own temperament is a mixture of warmth, generosity, kindness and of thin-skinned explosiveness. He has a huge library and collection of paintings, has been a drama coach, a producer and a writer and is still, in his late 50s, a fairly convincing sample of the untamed male.

Above left Anthony Quinn, Hollywood's roving Earth Father, still, in his late 50s, looking ready to venture forth on some unchartered sea.
Below left Rasputin, surrounded by his followers, at the decadent court of the Russian Empress Alexandra. His name, meaning immoral, was given to him because he preached that salvation depended on repentance and so it was therefore prudent for men to accumulate a good store of fleshly sins.

Rasputin's real name was Gregory Efimovitch Novikh (1871-1916). He was given the name Rasputin (meaning immoral) because he preached that salvation depended on repentance and that it was therefore prudent for men to accumulate a good store of fleshly sins. This doctrine was as attractive to the decadent court of St Petersburg as it had been to the Russian peasants among whom Rasputin first made his reputation. He was a kind of pre-Revolutionary hippy, a lanky, cadavorous figure with flowing hair, burning eyes and an extraordinarily compelling personality. Either through native cunning or hypnotic power, he managed to persuade the Empress Alexandra that he was a faith-healer who could save her haemophiliac son.

Rasputin, an illiterate Siberian fisherman, left his wife and small family in 1904, claiming divine inspiration, spent some time with the orgiastic Klisti order of monks and then began travelling widely and preaching throughout Russia. He was introduced to the court in 1906 and consolidated his hold over the Empress in 1912 when her 8-year-old son suffered agonising internal bleeding and appeared to be dying. Rasputin, who was then in Siberia, sent a telegram reassuring her. Immediately, the boy began to recover. (One explanation of this apparent miracle is that Rasputin had the ability to calm the neurotic Empress and this communicated itself to her son, whose bleeding was partly nervous).

Rasputin used his influence to promote his own friends at court and to interfere in affairs of State increasingly until 1916, when a group of nobles led by Prince Felix Youssoupoff murdered him in a St Petersburg house. His remarkable physical powers were demonstrated for the last time when he drank a huge dose of cyanide, was shot at point-blank range but still managed to crawl from the house until stopped by a final bullet. According to his own daughter, Rasputin was an intelligent, kindly pacifist who loved the common people and had only three long love affairs. This hardly corresponds with the legend of the baleful sensualist who was master of ceremonies at aristocratic orgies. Of his wife's political Svengali, the Emperor Nicholas unhappily remarked: "Better 20 Rasputins than one neurotic woman."

Johnny Ray, born John Alvin Ray was adored by millions between 1951 and 1956 for sobbing his heart out on stage. He was skinny, pallid and sunken-cheeked. He wore a deaf aid. He had baggy trousers and mousy hair slicked with water. He moved clumsily and hopped about the stage in a parody of grief, stamping his feet, hugging one knee to his stomach and turning his back on his audience to cry. Even his voice, he admitted, was "as flat as a billiard table". Yet he played to rapt, flushed, half-hysterical audiences and the record that made his name as the "Nabob of Sob" sold an amazing 2½ million – a single with "Cry" on one side and "The Little White Cloud" on the other.

His mission-hall childhood in Dallas, Oregon, where he was born in 1925, left him with an ear injury which reduced his hearing by 50 percent. He landed on the floor while being tossed in a blanket at the boys' club where he played the piano. The handicap suddenly cut him off from his friends and it was his ability to communicate his emotional hunger through his songs that seems to have been the key to his later success. He was an obscure club singer until the "Cry" record in 1951. During the next 10 years he made $1 million. His own explanation was that he sold "sincerity". He looked pathetic and audiences enjoyed yearning with him. He may have been a catalyst for suburban blues. Ray's own marriage to Marilyn Morrison in 1953 broke down, as did an engagement in 1955. He is still a moderately successful singer of heavy ballads on the US nightclub circuit.

Johnnie Ray, the "Prince of Wails", in his only film – "There's No Business Like Show Business" which he made in 1954. His best known single record was "Cry" which he made in 1951.

oobert Redford has a faintly chilling quality about him which sits oddly with his reddish-blonde Ivy-league good looks and may account for his extraordinary appeal to a generation for which coolness is everything. He projects a kind of quiet, deadpan recklessness, like someone who is always competing against himself in some remote and silent dare. The mood was unstated in "Butch Cassidy and the Sundance Kid" (1969) and more explicit in "Downhill Racer" the same year, in which Redford played a fiercely competitive skier. The hardness is real. Friends who have skied with him at "Sundance", the resort he is developing in Utah, say he likes goading them to take risks, test themselves. He jokes about himself as "the Kid" and like a perennial adolescent has always been restless and enjoyed winning. He may attract young audiences because in most of his films he makes other people look old. He seems to have an instinct for contemporary fashion as well.

Redford has three children and has been married since 1958 to a Mormon, Lola Jean. He was born in Santa Monica, California, in 1937, won a baseball scholarship to the University of Colorado in 1955 but soon dropped out. The restlessness that had led him into some juvenile hell-raising and hot-rodding, took him to Europe where he hitch-hiked and sold paintings to get by. He returned to study art and drama in 1958, won a walk-on Broadway role in 1959 and went into television, often playing neurotic killers. The play "Barefoot in the Park" suggested he might have a career as a light comedian, but he lost interest, went back to Europe with his family, and found his real screen personality only in "Butch Cassidy". He is a highly economical, intuitive actor who can suggest inner loneliness better than almost anyone else on the screen.

California born Robert Redford. His well known films include "Butch Cassidy and the Sundance Kid", "The Sting" and "The Great Gatsby".

Oliver Reed has a certain bull-like, scowling strength, and a look of brute sensuality rare among British actors, and irresistible, he claims, to women.

Oliver Reed irritated American pressmen in 1971 by telling them he was "Mr England" and that he was irresistible to women. But he does have a certain bull-like, scowling strength, a look of brute sensuality rare among British actors. In terms of the bawdy traditions of English smoking-room songs, he would be ideally cast as the local squire with the low desire – a strapping, brooding, lustful figure in riding breeches, stamping about in sullen search of virgins.

Reed lives up to at least part of this image by lording it in a huge mansion on a 50-acre property near Dorking where he lives with his girlfriend and small daughter.

Since his marriage to Kathleen Byrne (1960-70), he has been opposed to wedlock. He also dislikes women's liberationists. He was born in London in 1938, was a strip-club bouncer at 17, worked as a medical orderly and then got a small part in "The Rebel" (1960). Until "I'll Never Forget Whatisname" (1967), his most notable role was as a werewolf. But since then he has always looked a dynamic actor, needing only the right film to project himself as an international sex symbol in the Clark Gable tradition of male chauvinism.

Burt Reynolds as Lewis, the tough canoeist of the 1973 film, "Deliverance". His is the old appeal of a gentle and respectful nature in a burly physique; off-screen he has a considerable reputation as a comic.

urt Reynolds, of the mahogany tan, white teeth, black hair and bulging biceps, has been America's apostle of overt masculinity since 1972 when he took off all his clothes for *Cosmopolitan* magazine, covering himself only with a brawny forearm. However, he owes his huge following of 25 to 40-year-old women not to the fact that he was the coy first male nude but to a series of appearances on television talk shows which revealed a man of considerable humour and honesty. His is the old appeal of a gentle and respectful nature in a burly physique. The air of menacing overkill is counteracted by an extrovert ability to laugh at his own superstud image.

He has what he calls "the most ostentatious house in Hollywood" as well as a ranch in Florida. International success has come late in films like "Deliverance" (1972). But he has been a stuntman and actor since 1960 and for years played the Indian blacksmith of "Gunsmoke" on television. His grandmother was a full-blooded Cherokee. His father worked as a cowboy before joining the police

and becoming chief of the Palm Beach force. Burt was born in 1936. At Florida State College he played football well enough to consider a professional career in the game. An accident ended these hopes and in 1953 he won a drama award to study in New York. From 1963 to 1966 he was married to Judy Carne, the sock-it-to-me lady of "Laugh-In". It was she who suggested to *Cosmopolitan's* editor that Reynolds would be an ideal nude centrefold because he had "a great bottom". He agreed to do it without a fee as a send-up of the *Playboy* pin-ups. His droll, relaxed, self-deprecating approach to life came across when he and his ex-wife were guests on the Dick Cavitt show, since when he has become something of a society court-jester. For some years, his closest companion has been singer Dinah Shore who is 17 years older than him.

Baron Von Richtoven, revered in song, in movies and in the beagle dreams of the comic-strip character Snoopy, is celebrated as the last knight of the 20th Century. As war becomes more mechanized and inhuman, his legend grows, born of an era of wire-and-fabric flight in which men could still duel together in heroic single combat, high above the stench of the trenches. Fact is unlikely to intrude into the nostalgia that colours the Red Baron's story, lending him a chivalry that has obscured the real man.

Manfred Von Richtoven seems to have been an instinctive killer from childhood when he shot a tame duck on his father's estate in Prussia and displayed its tail feathers in his room. Initially, at least, he regarded war as an extension of souvenir hunting. He hung red, white and blue symbols, cut from downed British machines on the walls of his family home and had silver cups made to mark his first 60 kills (crafted, oddly enough, by a British silversmith). This custom was abandoned only after he had himself been wounded and shot down in July, 1917, an event which matured him and left him both with a premonition of death and with greater sympathy for his victims. The last pilot he shot down saw Richtoven waving when he stepped clear of the blazing wreck.

At the opening of World War I, fliers had given each other friendly waves as they passed. Later they flew side by side, potting each other with pistols or rifles. Richtoven himself, introduced the innovation of mounting a machine gun in front of the pilot as well as the tail-gunner. He had joined the air force because he had been unable to see who he was killing in the cavalry. When he passed his flying test (after two failures) in 1915, he was 25, a slim, blond, handsome nobleman who marked himself out for leadership not so much through flying skill as through fearlessness, stamina and an analytical approach to combat tactics. (He once demonstrated his stoicism by winning a cavalry steeplechase riding 45 miles with a broken collarbone).

As a man, he was cold, correct and somewhat insensitive. He had a mystery fiancée and used to amuse brother officers by reading aloud passionate letters other German girls sent him once his fame began to spread. His Jagdstaffel (hunting step) group began to dominate the Western Front in September, 1916, using the "circus" tactics which eschewed stunts in favour of efficiency. By attacking from a height with the sun behind him, Richtoven began accumulating a staggering number of kills, making three sorties a day and sometimes giving demonstrations of his skill for visiting generals. He won Germany's highest flying award, the Blue Max and became her most glamorous hero.

Though public adulation embarrassed him, Richtoven took his own legend seriously and had both his Albatross and the Fokker triplane he later flew, painted blood red so his enemies would know him. His 1917 crash made Germany aware of the damage to morale his loss might cause and he was pressured to give up flying. He himself seems to have lost confidence, but he refused to be grounded. Soon after his 80th kill he attacked a Canadian pilot whose squadron leader, Captain Roy Brown, tailed his Fokker and brought it down just in front of the Australian trenches. Richtoven was found with a bullet through his heart, still clutching the plane's joystick. He was buried with full military honours – a more romantic fate than befell his successor in command – Herman Goering.

Thousands of German schoolgirls pinned this photograph of Baron Von Richtoven on their walls. The legendary Red Baron, said to have been worth two infantry divisions, was the last knight of the 20th century.

Romeo's praise of Juliet at his first sight of her ''O, she doth teach the torches to burn bright'', captures the essence of the romantic tradition in literature. He is the last of the immortal lovers who include Paris, Troilus, Hero, Anthony, Launcelot, Paolo and Abelard. To all of them, love is a consuming lyrical passion, painful in its intensity, sweeping aside prudence and reason. If Romeo has become the exemplar of lovesick youth, it is probably because his passion was the rashest and most brief. In the play, he meets Juliet while in disguise at the ball of the Capulets, deadly rivals of his own family. They are secretly married and are together for only one soft Italian night before he is banished for killing her cousin, Tybalt in a duel. To rejoin him, Juliet feigns death. She wakes to find Romeo has swallowed poison beside her bier. ''Romeo and Juliet'' was the fruit of Shakespeare's own experience of love as a bewildering force which could have cruel consequences. Into the mouth of the friar (whose muddled planning causes the tragedy), Shakespeare put words that adults have been saying, in one form or another, to ardent adolescents ever since: ''These violent delights have violent ends.''

Romeo, the world's most famous balcony-climber, was a typical Elizabethan in his poetic ardour, but may also have reflected Shakespeare's own experience.

Omar Sharif as Zhivago and Julie Christie as Lara in the heavily romanticised 1965 film version of Boris Pasternak's great novel, "Dr Zhivago".

Omar Sharif, born Maechel Shalhoub, and known sometimes as "Cairo Fred", appeared in the film "Lawrence of Arabia" like a flame wavering far out in the desert, an eddy of colours shimmering and fusing slowly into the form of a horse and rider, the image solidifying finally into a lean-faced man with flashing dark eyes and silky brown hair. As an international star, Sharif has remained something of a mirage. Despite a gentle, soulful-eyed performance as Dr Zhivago in the 1966 film, he has never quite managed to become a wholly convincing romantic idol – possibly because he is too cool and detached to regard acting as anything more than a pastime and it shows.

He was born in Alexandria of Lebanese-Syrian parentage in 1932. His father was a wealthy timber merchant and he spent five years in the business himself before a friend offered him the lead in a 1954 film with Egypt's leading lady, Fatten Hamama. He became a Moslem to marry her the following year and, as Omar El Cherif, was in many Egyptian films. Since his marriage ended in 1966, he has lived mainly in Paris. Women's magazines (for whom he is an understandably popular interview subject) report that he is obsessed with "birds, bridge and bloodstock". As well as being a bridge player of international standard, he is a formidable chess player and a man of considerable elegance and charm.

Frank Sinatra, (born Francis Albert Sinatra) has more significantly changed our idea of what constitutes male attraction than any other man. One measure of the change is that Sinatra's appeal now seems fairly obvious. Thirty years ago it seemed astonishing.

"What the hell's that?" asked Benny Goodman, whirling round to face the audience at New York's Paramount Theatre on December 30, 1942. He had just casually introduced Frank Sinatra at the end of a show featuring the Goodman band and Peggy Lee. A scraggy 27-year-old walked on stage and hundreds of girls in the theatre began screaming. What is now par for the pop-star course was then a new phenomenon, baffling and disturbing. In the weeks that followed, as the show ran on and the lines of queueing bobby-soxers lengthened, newspaper columnists tried to come to grips with what was happening. What did Sinatra have? A good voice – like "slightly worn velveteen" one critic said. But this did not seem to explain the female hysteria that mounted throughout 1943 wherever Sinatra appeared and culminated in a near-riot in Times Square in the autumn of 1944. More than 500 police had to be brought in to control a crowd of nearly 30,000. Women were fainting, shrieking, fighting for his cigarette butts, putting band-aids on fingers that had touched his, nearly strangling the man with his own floppy bow tie.

"Not since Rudolph Valentino has American womanhood made such unabashed public love to an entertainer", said *Time* magazine. But whereas Valentino had dark, graceful good looks, Sinatra looked like the before part of a body-building course in how not to get sand kicked in your face. Hollow cheeks, big ears, spindly frame, a curl of thin dark hair flopping over a pale forehead, forceps scars on his neck. He stood clutching the microphone as if for support, hardly moving, a nervous smile quivering at one side of his mouth. The best explanation anyone could offer was that Sinatra summed up the hurt and the emotional hunger of a war-weary generation.

Some of the publicity put out about "Frankie's" background supported this image of deprivation. Hints of gang brawls in the tough port of Hoboken where he grew up with pin-ups of George Raft and Edward G. Robinson beside the photo of Bing Crosby on his wall. He had made the gruelling circuit of amateur talent contests, radio-station singing and local club work before being signed by first Harry James and then Tommy Dorsey as a lead singer in the big band era. By 1942 when he decided to go out on his own, he had already topped the *Downbeat* poll of singers and begun to grow away from the local girl he had married in 1939, Nancy Barbato.

The underdog image was partly true. Though his Italian-born parents were never on the breadline and though his own boyhood had been conventional enough, he had always had an affinity with people on the wrong side of society. "I think Sinatra's always had a secret desire to be a hood", Bing Crosby once said, hastily adding that he had too much class. Sinatra was certainly a crusader against prejudice long before this became a fashionable attitude. He had dumped a newspaperman who made an anti-Semitic remark at a party during his days with the Dorsey band. He was known as a hot-tempered man, a high-liver, a natty dresser – and a founding member of the Sinatra fan club. An RCA Victor recording chief remembers that when he cut his first solo disc in 1942 he "displayed no humility, phoney or real". Almost from the start, he believed he was the best singer in the world.

The combative, self-assertive part of his character was to carry Sinatra far beyond the image created by his publicity men who, in the mid-1940s, equipped him with tear-apart suits and paid girls to set off the chain-reaction screaming of his early concerts. The vulnerable bobby-soxers' idol was steadily padded out with more conventional masculine traits. Sinatra the social rebel. Sinatra the gutsy fighter. Sinatra the arrogant heel. Sinatra the great lover. Sinatra the broken-hearted loser. Sinatra the philanderer. And finally, Sinatra the father-figure – or perhaps more aptly, the Godfather.

The key to the complex character of Frank Sinatra is that he seems to be torn by a central conflict. The same ego that says to the world "love me" also says "don't lean on me". His bouts of publicity-seeking alternate with an intense desire for privacy. Hence his often-ugly feuds with pressmen. His relationships with women seem to follow the same pattern of attraction and rejection. The 1950 breakup of his marriage to Nancy, mother of his three children, followed a turbulent romance with Ava Gardner which left him bitter and guilty. Between their eventual brief marriage in 1951 and the equally doomed love affair with his third wife, Mia Farrow, in the late 1960s, Sinatra nevertheless managed to consolidate his image as a dominant, successful male. Not through the number of notable ladies he squired – Lauren Bacall, Dorothy Provine, Juliet Prowse, Jill St John – but through drawing on the resource that has always been at the heart of the Sinatra magnetism, his artistry.

In 1949, his career was entering a trough. There were film flops. His vocal chords were strained. The romantic ballads he had sung were being pushed out by a new, belting music he had little sympathy with. By 1951 he was nowhere in the charts behind Guy Mitchell, Johnnie Ray, Frankie Laine. His personal life was in ruins. Suddenly, he bounced back with a stunning performance as Maggio in the film "From Here to Eternity" and with other portrayals that showed the same spirit of human indestructibility. Then came the advent of the LP record.

"Being an 18-carat manic depressive and having lived a life of violent contradictions, I have an over-acute capacity for sadness as well as elation", Frank Sinatra confessed to an interviewer in 1963.

Against tender backings of strings and saxaphones he sang songs like ''My Funny Valentine'', ''They Can't Take That Away From Me'', ''Young at Heart'', and found a new audience that he would continue to hold through another two decades.

The comeback was as irresistible to women as his singing has always been. Apart from his eyes, which are an intense, almost hypnotic blue, it is his voice that is the core of Sinatra's sex appeal. The lyrics he holds, fondles and finally releases have an intimacy that nobody before Sinatra had achieved. Where Crosby had crooned with an effortless, detached buoyancy, Sinatra wanted his audience to be completely involved. His technique was based on a careful study of the emotional effect of textural contrast, colour and tempo. Vocally, he was the first to use the microphone as a sexual appendage. To go any further, those who followed him had to vulgarize the idea and wave the microphone about.

Sinatra's impeccable musical taste, his perfectionism, is the final, immensely attractive contradiction in

Sinatra under pressure from Kim Novak and Rita Hayworth in the 1957 musical, ''Pal Joey''. This famous entertainer has more significantly changed our idea of what constitutes male attraction than any other man. One measure of the change is that Sinatra's appeal now seems obvious, 30 years ago it seemed astonishing.

his personality. His cocky energy, the shrewd business sense that has made him one of the most powerful figures in American entertainment, has its unappealing side. But women are teased by the possibility that the sycophantic bodyguards who surround him, his liking for hip language, his vulgarity, his sharp clothes and mean temper, are no more than a cloak. Beneath lies a gentleman of ''endearing sweetness'' (according to Celeste Holm), a ''charmer, a ladies' man'' (Jill St John), an ''incurable romantic'' (Sinatra himself). Above all, someone who means what he says or sings. ''I'm honest'', he told *Playboy* magazine. ''An audience is like a broad. If you're indifferent, endsville.''

Mark Spitz won 7 gold medals for swimming at the Munich Olympics in August, 1972, and instantly became the world's No. 1 pin-up boy. Standing here in his Stars-and-Stripes briefs with his medallions hung like Grecian ornaments of youth and beauty around his neck he looked the way Olympic champions usually look only in posters – 6ft of lean, sleek, tanned masculinity with high cheekbones, thick dark hair and moustache and a

Mark Spitz instantly became the world's No 1 pin-up boy when he won 7 gold medals for swimming at the Munich Olympics, in August 1972. But after a year of fame he acknowledged it had been hard to cope with.

smile of paralysing whiteness. Americans flipped. There were congratulatory calls from the White House, film and television offers and a rush of fan·letters. Some of his team-mates were not so charmed. "It could have happened to a nicer guy", one is supposed to have quipped. The aggressive power that propelled him through the water had sometimes spilled over into arrogance out of the pool. He had been a brash loner almost since he began dominating schoolboy races in Santa Clara. In 1968, at Mexico City, his pride had been wounded when he collected only two gold medals (in the relays) after announcing that he would win six.

Mark Andrew Spitz was born in Modesto, California in 1950. He took to the water at eight and trained so hard that his Rabbi became worried that he might not be attending to his lessons. Spitz's father is supposed to have reassured him that "Even God likes a winner". At the time of Munich, Mark was a pre-dental student at Indiana University. His moustache was barely dry from the Olympic pool before a razor company was offering him thousands of dollars to shave with their product – the beginning of a flood of commercial propositions arranged by his business agent, Norman Brokau, which were designed to earn Spitz $5 million in two years. He endorsed everything from suits to snorkels. But hopes that he might have enough sexual magnetism for a film career were dashed by some rather colourless appearances on television. After a year of wealth and fame, Spitz acknowledged that it had been hard to cope with. With his beautiful wife, Susan Weiner, he decided to concentrate on business.

James (Jimmy) Stewart was not the most handsome, graceful, poised and articulate man in films and the public loved him because he wasn't. The beanpole 6ft 4in frame, the dangling hands, the puzzled grey eyes, the long jaw and the drawling voice, had their own charm. He built a whole career on awkwardness combined with lump-in-the-throat determination.

James Maitland Stewart was born in 1908 in Pennsylvania where his father ran a hardware store. He was thin, wore glasses and dabbled in magic as well as chemistry and radio. He also played the accordion. After taking an architectural degree at Princeton in 1932, he drifted into the theatre, won a Broadway lead in 1934 and went to Hollywood with his friend, Henry Fonda, in 1935. "You Can't Take It With You" made him a star in 1938 and in the following year, "Mr Smith Goes To Washington" and "Destry Rides Again" (with Marlene Dietrich) established the homespun Stewart hero. He was a wish-fulfilment fantasy – the earnest young man whose naivety might make a fool of him in the first reel but who usually wound up with the best-looking girl in the fade-out. The explosions of bumbling courage that confounded crooked politicians and flinty financiers in his films of the

1930s were translated to the West during the 1950s and 60s when Stewart often played a diffident cowpoke roused to stubborn anger.

Some of the nervous quality that comes across in his films is real. As an actor and as a businessman-rancher, Stewart works hard, takes life fairly seriously and is something of a worrier. But his screen clumsiness is only a good act. During World War II he flew B24s and emerged a much-decorated Colonel who was later promoted to Brigadier-General. He was Hollywood's most famous bachelor until 1949 when he married Gloria McLean, becoming stepfather to her two children and father of two more.

Who else but James Stewart would find himself caught in a steamy bathroom with the door knob in his hand? He is seen here in a scene from his 1962 film comedy, "Mr Hobbs Takes a Vacation".

Tarzan, the chest-thumping ape-man of popular parody is a travesty of Tarzan as Edgar Rice Burroughs envisaged him when he first appeared in the *All Story* pulp magazine in October, 1912. To his creator, who was an Anglophile, he represented all the virtues Burroughs saw in the finest type of Englishman – strength, courage, freedom, justice, cleanliness, honesty and square-jawed, clear-eyed physical perfection.

In the original story of "Tarzan and the Apes", Lord Greystoke and his wife are castaways on the coast of Africa. After his wife dies, Lord Greystoke is killed by a band of great apes and their baby son, John Clayton, is snatched up and mothered by Kala. As Tarzan, he rises to kingship of the tribe of Kerchak. Far from being a sexual he-man, Tarzan was something of a prude with a narcissistic interest in his own physique. In "The Return of Tarzan" (1915), Burroughs married him off to Jane Porter whom he had rescued from the clutches of an ape rival, Terkoz. He was introduced to sensual temptation only in 1931 when he rejected the lascivious Queen of Cathne in "Tarzan and the City of Gold". (Burroughs' own marriage had broken up at the time over his infatuation with an actress, Thelma Todd). The following year, the reign of Johnny Weismuller began as MGM's Tarzan, Weismuller, who had won Olympic Swimming medals in 1924 and 1928, was to swing, vault and thresh about more impressively than any other Tarzan in a jungle MGM built around the shores of Toluca Lake, North Hollywood.

Burroughs had been born in Chicago in 1875, was an ex-cavalry officer, and had been selling advertisements for magazines when he decided, at the age of 36, to try his hand at a story about Mars. The idea of Tarzan the following year was suggested by Mowgli of Kipling's *Jungle Book.* An incredibly prolific and imaginative writer, Burroughs produced 26 Tarzan books without ever visiting Africa. The Tarzan films began in 1918, starring Elmo Lincoln. In 1929, the ape man swung into comics in a revolutionary series of strip panels. Hal Foster had designed to do away with balloon captioning. Rex Mason carried on the comic and it is possibly in this form that Tarzan has made his greatest impact as a folk hero. Burroughs, who died in 1950, did not live to see the resurgence of interest in his hero during the 1960s when Tarzan books became runaway best-sellers in paperbacks. In the age of technology and urban neuroses, Tarzan's physical splendour and his willingness to depend on his own strength and skill have made him a naive but enduring symbol of the noble primitive.

Opposite, upper left *The original Tarzan, Johnny Weismuller, in "Tarzan and his Mate" made in 1934.*
Bottom left *Mike Henry having a little trouble with an unfriendly native in "Tarzan's Golden Safari".*
Right *Lex Barker, the star of 5 Tarzan movies.*

Robert Taylor, playing an American World War I officer, with Vivien Leigh in "Waterloo Bridge" (1940) – the film made many Americans feel bad about not being in the war.

Robert Taylor had all the necessary assets to become a heart-throb except his name – Spangler Arlington Brough. The MGM studio fixed that soon after a talent scout had sighted him in a college play in 1933 (he was studying medicine). He picked a screen name from a "suitable list" and made his first appearance in "Handy Andy" in 1934. His widow's peak of black hair, his dark blue eyes, his fine profile, his gentle voice and impeccable manners made him the favourite leading man of a succession of screen beauties whom he escorted through long passages of purple dialogue with all the romantic tact of a professional dancing partner.

Taylor was the son of a Nebraska grain merchant. He was a conservative man who gave the gossip columnists no ammunition. After his 1939 marriage to Barbara

Stanwyck ended in 1951, he married the German actress, Ursula Theiss and they had two children. He liked hunting, shooting, fishing and sounding off about communism. By the time of his death (from lung cancer) he had seen his own carefully-combed style of masculinity swept away by a vogue for more rugged heroes. But in the late 1930s, he was named "the most handsome man in America". He never saw himself as a great actor and once told the *Harvard Lampoon* he was delighted to receive their Oscar as worst actor, for "Quo Vadis". But he could project considerable quiet charm – notably in "A Yank at Oxford" (1938) and "Waterloo Bridge" (1940). He was probably the last successful matinee idol.

Spencer Tracy was an unlikely candidate as a heart-throb. He had about as much glamour as an oak barrel. During the 1930s, when he sometimes co-starred with Clark Gable, it was always Gable who got the girl. But as time weathered him, Tracy became his own legend of the American male as a husband-figure, a father-figure and finally, in films like "Judgement at Nuremberg", a grandfather-figure. Nobody was surprised when the Women's Research Guild in 1950 named him "the man who most strongly influences women emotionally." Tracy was a heart-throb of a unique kind.

The pugnacious jaw, the bitten lips, the long, disgusted glare, the sudden warmth and blinked-back tears that were the trademarks of Tracy's style on the screen were also the manifestations of an emotional Irish temperament. Tracy could be gregarious, tolerant and humorous. He could also be irritable, selfish and impatient. For some years after he arrived in Hollywood he was the unruliest drinker and biggest trouble-maker in the film community. He was born in Milwaukee in 1900. His father, a carrier, hoped he might become a priest. But Spencer couldn't wait to leave his Jesuit school and at 17 was in the navy. He later went back to college where he found he could express his dynamic and restless temperament on the stage. He graduated from the American Academy of Dramatic Arts in 1923 and the same year married Louise Treadwell, the leading lady of the first stock company he joined. The birth of a deaf son, John, the following year began the fluctuations between moroseness and high spirits that were to mark his career from then on.

After a huge success as the tough hero of "The Last Mile" on the stage in 1930, he moved into films. He fell painfully in love with Loretta Young in 1933, but went back to his wife a year later after Miss Young announced that their Catholic beliefs would never allow them to marry. Off-screen, Tracy became a hell-raiser, once falling asleep on the set of a film he was making and drunkenly wrecking it when he woke in the middle of the night. On-screen, he became the man's man hero of films like "Captain's Courageous" (1937) and Hollywood's best-known screen priest, winning his second successive Oscar for his playing of Father Flanagan in "Boys' Town" (1938).

Tracy's reputation as a woman's man began to develop only in his 40s after he and Katherine Hepburn began sparring affectionately in "Woman of the Year" (1942). Miss Hepburn has described the script rules of the series of comedies they made together over the next few years: "The woman is always pretty sharp. She needles the man a little, like a mosquito. Then he slowly puts out his big paw and slaps the lady down." Though part of his appeal was his perpetual boyishness, Tracy always looked as if he knew how to handle women. When Hepburn met him she is supposed to have said: "I fear I may be too tall for you Mr Tracy." To which he answered: "Don't worry Miss Hepburn. I'll soon cut you down to size." They loved each other for more than 20 years in a dignified, never-publicized relationship which lasted until Tracy's death in 1967. During much of this time, he lived alone in a spartan cottage on the estate of director George Cukor, grown white and solitary and seldom leaving his books, his music and his painting. All his heart, body and guts had gone into the creation of a screen personality as solid and comforting as a crag.

Spencer Tracy and Katherine Hepburn – a friend called them a "collective personality". On one film, Tracy stopped work because Hepburn had her feet on a chair, and he knew, without looking, when she had removed them.

ierre Trudeau – "He's runty, pock-marked and his hair is getting thin, but he radiates like hell", said one of his campaign managers. The assessment does less than justice to the physical attraction of this remarkable man.

With its mobile features, humorous, bruised-looking eyes, crooked grin and small ears laid close to a neat skull, Trudeau's face (pitted by teenage acne) has a faun-like charm which would look more at home in a French film than a legislative chamber. In combination with wit, intelligence, athleticism and non-conformity, Trudeau's political power as Prime Minister of Canada provides him with a fairly lethal combination of male assets. To the disgust of political opponents, the Trudeau panache extends even to his family life – his wife, Margaret, gave birth to their first child, Justin, on Christmas Day. When he married in March, 1971, Canadian teenagers lowered their school flags to half-mast. Trudeau was 51, his vivacious wife, 22. Nobody felt he was too old for her.

What marks Trudeau out from more run-of-the-mill photogenic politicians is that his magnetism is totally unconventional. "The only constant factor to be found in my thinking over the years has been opposition to accepted opinions", he has said. There is an abrasiveness in Trudeau which women appreciate rather more than the Canadian electorate, which nearly dislodged his Government in the 1972 election. The touch of intellectual arrogance, his unwillingness to suffer fools gladly, his candidness and "cool" are the stuff of sexual, not political, "machismo".

Pierre Eliot Trudeau was born in 1920, inherited a fortune, along with mixed Scots-French blood, when his father died in 1935 after making money in land and oil, attended a French Jesuit college in Montreal, then Harvard, the London School of Economics and the Sorbonne. This formidable academic background was enlivened by a world tour in the course of which he managed to get himself arrested three times – in the Khyber Pass, in Arab Jerusalem and off the Florida coast while trying to paddle a canoe to Cuba. After launching a left-wing intellectual journal and becoming law professor at Montreal University, he entered politics in 1965, seeing a danger of Canada being pulled apart by its French-English tensions. He was forceful and dynamic and rose fast to succeed Lester Pearson as leader of the Liberal Party.

During the 1968 election, the rather austere, even monkish side of Trudeau's character was submerged in the making of a jet-set playboy image. There were articles about his karate, his skin-diving, his motor-cycling and his fondness for hippy discotheques and beautiful women. A champion of private morality ("The State has no business in the bedrooms of the nation"), he had shrugged off earlier reflections cast on his masculinity at the time when he was introducing homosexual law

Canada's Prime Minister, Pierre Trudeau, sporting a tie few other Premiers would, or could, wear. Equally bold on the ski slopes, he took on the Cresta Run in a one-man bob sled at the age of 53.

reform. Now he was seen about with a dazzling array of partners, including Barbra Streisand, model Melita Clark, actress Jennifer Eale and television announcer Dianne Giguere. Interviewed by *Time* magazine, Trudeau confessed that his three most exciting experiences were his first love-making, his first solo flight and his first scuba dive.

The emphasis on glamorous recreations and sex-appeal led one wit to say when Trudeau was elected: "He looks fantastic, but will he work?" The other side of Trudeau, however, is a highly-disciplined, cold and confident intelligence. More recently, he has flirted less with the electorate, stopped worrying about the thinning hair he used to comb forward in a Caesar cut, and got to grips with the economic and racial problems that press any Canadian Government hard. With his dry humour, his informality and his off-beat political style, Trudeau is what one Canadian woman called "the sexiest thing ever to hit politics".

A romantic, 19th century impression of a dashing Dick Turpin daringly clearing the Hornsey toll gate, on Black Bess, to the consternation of the law.

Dick Turpin reflects the urge to romanticise the outlaw which is irresistible in the case of the highwayman. His crimes were accomplished with some style and his victims were usually people who could afford to lose the jewels and purses he carried off into the night. His ''stand and deliver'' and the thunder of hoofs as he raced off into the night were a bold contrast with the sneakiness of pickpockets and back-alley thugs. It is not surprising that some gentlemen of the road became sex heroes. What is surprising is that Dick Turpin should have emerged as the most famous of them.

The Turpin of folklore is the highwayman who rode Black Bess to York, pursued by the law and cheered on by common folk – a story popularized in the 19th Century romantic novel *Rookwood* by Harrison Ainsworth. The Turpin of reality was a pock-marked killer and rapist who was hanged for horse-stealing at the Mount, York, on April 7, 1739. He was born in England about 1708 at Hempstead, Essex, where his father was a butcher and tavern-keeper. He set up as a butcher himself at Thaxted in 1728 after marrying Betty Millington, but was soon in trouble for stealing cattle, smuggling and thieving. For one crime, in which a farmer was scalded with boiling water and his maid raped, Turpin's companions were hanged. He himself jumped to freedom from an alehouse window and took to the road with another highwayman, Tom King. They built a hideout in Epping Forest, became the most feared highwaymen on the north-eastern approaches to London, and for a year or two lived high, wore fine clothes and were welcomed at local inns with warm beds, wine and women.

They were finally betrayed, King was wounded, and Turpin retreated to Yorkshire, where he and his wife tried to establish themselves as country gentry. Turpin aroused the suspicion of a hunting companion when he threatened to shoot someone. He was bound over by a magistrate and unmasked after a letter he sent to his brother at Hempstead was recognized at the post office there by his old school-teacher and traced back to York. On the scaffold, he stamped his right leg to stop it trembling, chatted amiably with the hangman and then flung himself into space – and into legend.

Rudolph Valentino wrote, "Love is honey. It is a flower. It may be fierce as a tiger-lily. But it must be beautiful, delicate, gentle, too." The author of these passinale phrases has a unique place in cinema history. He appeared just after films had advanced beyond their developmental stage and just before Victorian repressions were swept away in the 1920s. Thanks to this coincidence of timing, Valentino became the phantom lover of thousands of American women who were mesmerised by the image they saw on the silver screen. There could never again be a heart-throb quite so purple, produced in quite such a hothouse sexual climate.

The contrast between Valentino and his screen image is remarkable. In "The Sheik", he came across as a kind of thrilling menace. Bogus studio biographies gave him a faintly aristocratic background. But in fact he was a likeable, rather unaggressive Italian farm boy. His real name was Rololpho Guglielmi (he added the name Di Valentina about 1915) and he was born in 1895 at Castellaneta, Southern Italy. His father, a peasant with some veterinary training, died when he was 11 and Rodolpho was an unruly teenager who did not seem likely to settle down to village life. In 1913, his uncles shipped him by steerage to New York where he worked as a gardener on a Long Island estate. He would later claim he had graduated from an agricultural college and that he was hired to landscape the estate. What does seem certain is that he made a careful study of the manners of the rich young men he saw on Long Island and used what he learned to make himself a charming dance partner for New York socialites who went to Maxim's cabaret.

His tango style and dark good looks caught the eye of cafe dancer Bonnie Glass, who took him on tour. His next dance partner, Joan Sawyer, fired him when he implicated her in a messy divorce action brought against businessman Jack De Samuels by his wife, Bianca, who, a year later, shot her ex-husband. Rodolpho hurried off to the West Coast, leaving behind a murky incident in which the police had arrested him on suspicion of blackmail. The files on this case are now empty and Valentino later dismissed the affair as a frame-up, which it probably was. In Hollywood between 1917 and 1919, he had a fairly undistinguished career dancing in musicals and playing small parts as a villain. He fitted the current stereotype – dark, foreign and therefore sinister. An actress, Jean Acker, married him in 1919 but changed her mind the moment the wedding party was over and locked him out of her bedroom. A more influential woman had, however, noticed his extraordinarily photogenic quality – scenario writer June Mathis. She arranged for him to play Julio, the Argentinian hero of "The Four Horsemen of the Apocalypse" (1920) and the off-beat casting was an immense success.

Valentino's impact in "The Sheik", the following year was even greater. "His acting", said producer Adolph Zukor, "is largely confined to protruding his large almost occult eyes until the vast areas of white are showing, drawing back the lips of his wide, sensuous mouth to bare his gleaming teeth and flaring his nostrils". Women were not so critical. Valentino was different from any screen lover they had seen. He kissed with Latin directness and enjoyment. His gallantry was unselfconscious and he moved with superb grace. In 1921, the sight of an Arab chieftain jerking an Englishwoman on to his saddle, streaking across the sands with burnoose flapping to his desert lair and there overwhelming her with burning looks and animal ferocity created a sensation.

The image of the masterful conqueror was an illusion. Valentino himself was sitting at home patiently courting Natacha Rambova. She was a beautiful, pretentious American woman (real name Winifred Shaughnessy Hudnut) who had given up a dancing career to indulge a flair for designing high-camp scenery. Rambova tried to take over Valentino's career and dedicate it to her concept of Art and Beauty. Her ambitions led to a bitter struggle with the studios. Valentino did not work for nearly two years and had a frustrating time trying to divorce Jean Acker (a marriage which had never been consummated) and wed Rambova. Before his new marriage became legal he was threatened with conviction as a bigamist and ordered to live apart from Rambova for a year. And at the end of this struggle, another humiliation waited. Rambova lost interest in him when the studios grew tired of her interference and cut her out of any further say in his career. Left on his own again, the bewildered Valentino made a manful attempt to live up to the rakish image the public had of him. He spent wildly, dressed ostentatiously, drove cars recklessly and was seen about with exotic stars like Pola Negri. He was deeply hurt when a columnist, irritated by the installation of powder machines in men's toilets, blamed Valentino for a trend towards effeminacy. The Great Lover issued a boxing challenge and was seen displaying his powerful build in a sparring session with Jack Dempsey.

In 1926, after filming another romantic aphrodisiac, "The Son of the Sheik", Valentino suddenly contracted an infection from a perforated ulcer and ruptured appendix. Within a week, he was dead. Worship of his image now took on morbid overtones as thousands of distraught women fought to see his body. Pola Negri staged a well-publicized collapse. Rambova herself encouraged the Valentino cult with revelations of his psychic powers and messages from the spirit world. There were more clear-eyed appraisals of Valentino and his strange attraction. The critic H.L. Mencken, who met him soon before his death, found him boysihly naive and "respectable". He was touched by his predicament: "Here was one who was catnip to women. Here was one who had youth and fame. And here was one who was very unhappy."

Valentino's physical attributes were part of his ap-

A rare shot of Rudolph Valentino in primitive mood, one of a number of publicity stills he made for "The Faun through the Ages" which was never filmed.

peal – his symmetrical Roman features, his patent-leather hair, his dancer's hidden strength, his flashing teeth and mournful eyes with their hypnotic circles of white. His brooding air was intensified by a dead nerve which made one eyelid droop. All this was overlaid with the exotic sensuality suggested by his film roles and his publicized views on love. These presented him either as a Casanova wise in the ways of European gallantry, as a fatal lover (the bullfight of "Blood and Sand") or as a fiery Arab with thrilling connotations of polygamy. Valentino provided an escape from the dull conventions of American boy-meets-girl relationships and from the tedium of marriages in which the woman's sexual needs were little understood. It was morally safe for women to imagine themselves in the Sheik's arms because he abducted his co-stars, overcame their maidenly scruples with brute force. There was no shilly-shallying. To the question "Why have you brought me here?" he answered "Are you not woman enough to know?" At the same time, women could sense that this beautiful, menacing lover would also be sympathetic to desires they could express to nobody else.

Jon Voight hamming for the camera – he has the looks and screen personality to represent a new type of sex symbol, the handsome male as victim rather than hero.

Jon Voight, like Marlon Brando, is one of the few actors who has pinned down a whole male species in his first film with his portrayal of Joe Buck, the narcissistic sex adventurer of ''Midnight Cowboy'' (1969). The film explored the irony of a beautiful, stupid youth who believes in the Western myth of manhood and sees himself as God's gift to the women of New York until the city reduces him from would-be stud to mere bait for homosexuals.

Voight has the looks and screen personality to represent a new type of sex symbol – the handsome male as victim rather than conqueror. Though he is tall, blonde, muscular and square-jawed, his round grey eyes seem to startle and take fright in a peculiarly vulnerable way. He was born in New York in 1939, is the son of a golf professional, graduated from the Catholic University and had won critical awards off Broadway before being

picked for ''Midnight Cowboy'' on the recommendation of his girl-friend, Jennifer Salt, who was the daughter of the screenplay writer. Voight was formerly married to actress Laurie Peters.

John Wayne had less charm than Gary Cooper, but he has turned out to be the most durable Western hero of them all. He was top at the box office after ''Red River'' in 1949 and was top again after ''True Grit'' more than 20 years later, at the age of 62. This thin-lipped grin, his monotone voice, his flat-lidded eyes, his beefsteak hands and 6ft 4in bulk have the unchanging, solid quality of a tree, embedded like a landmark on the Hollywood

John Wayne in mid-career. He told a 1974 TV audience he had made about 200 Westerns and would be happy to forget 170 of them.

horizon. His screen presence is so real that he barely needs to act at all.

Wayne is a male type without nuances. He is invariably tough to men and gentle to women. He doesn't pursue them; they come to him. If they misbehave he simply spanks their bottoms. He is always stoical, always self-reliant. His virility is based not on aggression but on endurance. He administers his own justice with hard-nosed cynicism ''Due process of law is a bullet'', he says in ''The Green Berets''. The star image and the man have become so inseparable that it is hard now to see him as Marion Michael Morrison, son of an Iowa druggist, who had to be taught how to say ''aint'' like a Westerner when he first went to films in 1930. He was born in 1907 and had come to Hollywood from the University of California where he was more used to throwing football passes than roping steers. His break from B-grade Westerns came in 1939 with John Ford's historic ''Stagecoach''. Ten years later, the rangy, smooth-faced;

chivalrous young hero of that film had changed into a Western version of Captain Bligh – the hard-bitten, ruthless cattle baron of ''Red River''.

The autocratic personality was close to Wayne's own. Off-screen, he is ''the Duke'', a larger-than-life character in his drinking capacity, his physical hardness (he threw off lung cancer in the mid-1960s and boasted: ''I licked the Big C'') and his patriotism, which is of the illiberal George Wallace variety. He has had three marriages, all to small, graceful, exotic-looking women, and seven children (four by his Catholic first wife, Josephine, and three by his Peruvian third wife, Pilar). His enduring popularity is proof that the big, tough ''loveable hunk'' hasn't gone out of fashion as a folk hero.

evgeni Yevtushenko, a modern poet-hero reflected something more than the glamour of his lean good looks when his first tour of the West in 1961, became a triumphal progress. He would spread out his arms, raise his large blue eyes and shout his vehement verses and in Germany, France, Britain and America, audiences who could not understand a word of what he was saying, responded like teenagers confronted by a pop idol. He symbolized, for a time, the world's longing for an end to the Cold War, a token that Khrushchev's Russia was different from Stalin's.

Yevtushenko was born in 1933 in Siberia where his Ukranian grandfather had been exiled for setting fire to a landlord's estate. He was expelled from school (on a false charge), worked as a labourer for his geologist father and then went to Moscow where he began writing lyrical free verse in defiance of the anti-Semitic literary establishment. Students made him their hero and hoisted him to the platform on Poetry Day, 1961. Though he had been attacked in the Soviet Press only months before, Khrushchev allowed him to tour the West. It seemed that times were changing. Yevtushenko was handsome, jaunty, high-spiritied, impulsive. He liked jazz and the Twist. He was a natural showman with a rich baritone

John Wayne is a male type without nuances. Invariably tough to men he is gentle to women and his virility is based not on aggression but on endurance.

Yevtushenko in the early 1960s. A modern poet-hero lionised in the West but often under attack from the Kremlin for his "anarchic individualism".

voice and a blinding smile. And he was lionised everywhere.

In the years since then, some of his glamour has faded. Criticism in Russia of his "fantastic egocentricity" seemed to sap the intensity of his protest against blind obedience to the State. At Khrushchev's suggestion, he toned down *Babi-Yar,* his poem commemorating Russian Jews massacred by the Nazis near Kiev. Much of his semi-journalistic verse seemed to push the official Russian line. The enigma of Yevtushenko is whether this reflects prudent caution – his own wife's parents died in Stalin's labour camps – or whether the youthful rebel of the 1960s is turning into the party hawk of the 1970s.

miliano Zapata was the ideal answer to Marlon Brando's quest. Looking around for a vehicle in which he could portray a rebel hero, it is not surprising that, in 1952 he should have chosen "Viva Zapata". The film of Zapata's life was hardly more romantic than the reality of his 10-year struggle against social injustice in Mexico. He was a man of intriguing contradictions and of great "machismo", both politically and sexually. Many mistresses wept when he was trapped in a courtyard and shot by a supposed "honour guard" in April, 1919.

Emiliano Zapata shortly before his death in 1919. Marlon Brando achieved an astonishing physical resemblance in the 1952 film, ''Viva Zapata''.

Zapata had a shrewd sense of humour. When he first met President Madero to discuss Mexico's political future, he demonstrated his political concepts simply by presenting a gun to him and taking his watch. Madero came to power in 1910 after the fall of Diaz, against whose tyranny Zapata had led a peasant revolt in his home state of Morelos. He had been born in Anenecuilco in 1880 of a well-respected family a cut above the peasant class, and had taken the peasants' side against plantation owners who were grabbing land. His own revolt was matched in the north by a wilder uprising led by Pancho Villa.

Though he initially agreed to cooperate with Madero, who was a liberal, Zapata became disillusioned and went ahead with forcible reforms in Morelos, burning haciendas and eventually joining Villa in seizing power in Mexico City itself. Their partnership soon broke up and Zapata returned to Morelos where he carried on violent reform, ruling with a bandit army. He was decoyed to his death by a promise of arms from the Government. But his image as ''father of the revolution'' survived, and his Ayala Plan (which proposed giving a third of plantation land to the peasants) was successfully carried on by Zapatismo politicians.

Index